Arms and
African Development

edited by
Frederick S. Arkhurst

Published for the
Adlai Stevenson Institute
of International Affairs

The Praeger Special Studies program—
utilizing the most modern and efficient book
production techniques and a selective
worldwide distribution network—makes
available to the academic, government, and
business communities significant, timely
research in U.S. and international economic, social, and political development.

Arms and African Development

Proceedings of the First Pan-African Citizens' Conference

Praeger Publishers   New York Washington London

PRAEGER PUBLISHERS
111 Fourth Avenue, New York, N.Y. 10003, U.S.A.
5, Cromwell Place, London S.W.7, England.

Published in the United States of America in 1972
by Praeger Publishers, Inc.

Library of Congress Catalog Card Number: 70-182985

Printed in the United States of America

THE ADLAI STEVENSON INSTITUTE

The Adlai Stevenson Institute of International Affairs was founded in 1967 as a memorial to the late Governor Adlai Stevenson, former U.S. Ambassador to the United Nations. It is a private, non-partisan non-profit organization financed solely by contributions from private sources—individuals, foundations and a consortium of universities. In order to safeguard its independence and avoid conflicts of interest, the Institute does not solicit or accept funds from any government.

The focus of the Institute's work is in the field of international political, social and economic development. As an action- and problem-oriented body, it seeks, within its limited financial resources, to assist in finding solutions to critical problems. The Institute's activities revolve around a group of high-caliber Fellows from various parts of the world and issues which, in its opinion, offer the best prospects of concrete solutions to specific problems of development. The Institute allows Fellows to develop projects of many kinds; from the creation of pilot projects in developing countries, to the preparation of teaching curricula and other action-oriented research.

In addition to its Board of Directors, the Institute has an International Council, with Lady Jackson (Barbara Ward) as its Chairman.

The 1970 Pugwash Conference on Science and World Affairs convened at Lake Geneva, Wisconsin, under the auspices of the Adlai Stevenson Institute of International Affairs and the American Academy of Sciences. The Pugwash movement attempts to bring together periodically scientists and scholars from all parts of the world for frank and informal exchange of views on various pressing international problems. Although the main conferences have been attended by scientists from the developing countries and study groups and small conferences have been devoted to specific problems of international scientific cooperation and development, the objective appears not to have been to elicit a Third World perspective on the activities and especially the agenda of the main conferences. This was, perhaps, understandable, since the genesis of Pugwash was the exploration of possible means of controlling the nuclear-arms race and minimizing the chances of the outbreak of nuclear war at the height of the cold war. Since that time, however, there has been increased emphasis on the importance of the problems of the developing world to long-range international stability.

It was the Adlai Stevenson Institute's view that a better perspective could be gained by having scholars and scientists from at least a part of the developing world react to the agenda of the main conference in the context of their own national and, in particular, regional problems. This was the basis of the African Regional Symposium on Disarmament and Development, which convened at the University of Ghana on July 28-31, 1970, under the sponsorship of the Adlai Stevenson Institute, the Ghana Academy of Arts and Sciences, and the University of Ghana. Beyond this immediate objective, it was hoped that the symposium would be the means of developing a permanent informal body of African scholars and scientists whose regular deliberations and possible linkage with the Pugwash movement would help to broaden the dimensions of the Pugwash conferences.

It is most gratifying to the sponsors of the symposium that the achievements of the first African symposium went beyond original expectations. Not only were the papers before the symposium of high caliber, but the discussions were extremely frank and realistic. Most important, the symposium decided to establish itself as a permanent body that would attract scientists and scholars from all of Africa—especially from the two linguistic zones—and to seek affiliation

with the Conference on Science and World Affairs. The sponsors'
only regret was that the participation by delegations from French-
speaking African countries was disappointing, even though several
of them had been invited. All the sponsors wish to acknowledge their
indebtedness to the Charles F. Kettering Foundation for its financial
support, which made the symposium possible.

The papers presented are offered in this volume, together with
an abridged and edited version of the proceedings, in the hope that it
will be of interest to those public and private bodies that the symposium decided should receive its main conclusions and recommendations.

Frederick S. Arkhurst

We in Ghana believe that education should be a cross-cutting experience transcending national boundaries and engaging the cooperative efforts not only of individuals within a nation but also of national and international institutions. This idea is implicit in the associations developed by the University of Ghana and the Ghana Academy of Arts and Sciences. The African Regional Symposium on Disarmament and Development is an example of the cooperation between international institutions that, I think, must be the basis for the development of a unifying world order—today, the most hopeful avenue for the assurance of the survival of the civilized human community.

It has been suggested—and I think quite rightly—that the new nations of Africa and Asia are the most ardent supporters of the United Nations and also the strongest advocates of a world order. The reasons are obvious. Our nations came into being partly as a result of the international atmosphere created by the authority of the United Nations. As small and developing nations that neither possess nor desire immense military establishments for the maintenance of national sovereignty or the guarantee of territorial integrity, we have to depend on the rule of law in the international community as the best assurance of our independence. Thus, perhaps, we have a fuller realization of the indispensability of a just and stable international order within which we can develop our potential. It is our belief that the most effective way of achieving such an order lies in constant interchange among nations, peoples, and groups as a means of breaking down the barriers of race, culture, religion, and prejudice and in establishing those lines of communication that can lead to a commonality of objectives among the peoples of the world.

The Adlai Stevenson Institute of International Affairs, I think, shares this view of the world order as indispensable to human progress. Certainly, its members perceive the problem of development, social change, and the establishment of a quality of life consistent with human dignity in a transnational context. It is thus most appropriate that the Institute should have conceived and sponsored this symposium

---

At the time of writing, William Ofori-Atta was Minister of Education in Ghana.

to investigate and deliberate upon problems of international concern within an African context.

The rising expenditures on arms throughout the world have a direct inhibiting effect on economic and social development, whether we are talking in terms of the experience of the United States, the Soviet Union, or the nations of Africa. This is a transnational problem, but because of the magnitude and potential cataclysmic results of arms competition among the superpowers the impact of arms expenditures in developing countries has not received adequate attention. The symposium, I hope, will do signal service by illuminating some aspects of this problem as they affect Africa. Even more important will be the emphasis given to the role of science and technology in African development in general and regional development in particular. It is now a widely held belief that meaningful African development must be predicated on closer coordination and integration of the African economies. Indeed, effective African industrialization can succeed only on the basis of large integrated markets in Africa itself. This realization poses an exciting and immensely difficult challenge for the African nations. It is my hope that the deliberations on the priorities for balanced economic development set before us here will provide valuable insights for all of us.

I am pleased to welcome to the symposium so many scientists and scholars from all over Africa. I am no less pleased to welcome our friends from the United States, whose contribution has been invaluable in making this meeting possible. We are especially indebted to the Charles F. Kettering Foundation of Dayton, Ohio, whose financial support was indispensable in bringing the symposium into being. My appreciation of the efforts of the University of Ghana and the Ghana Academy of Arts and Sciences in cosponsoring the symposium, of course, goes without saying.

In opening this symposium, I bring you the good wishes of the Ghana Government and the people of Ghana for a constructive and successful conference.

CONTENTS

PART IV: REVIEW OF THE SYMPOSIUM

8   REVIEW OF THE SYMPOSIUM

LIST OF TABLES

I

DISARMAMENT
AND
AFRICAN
DEVELOPMENT

1

A BRIEF
SURVEY OF
DISARMAMENT
NEGOTIATIONS

Frederick S. Arkhurst

While mass conflict and war are as old as the earliest settled human communities, disarmament and disarmament negotiations are associated with more recent times and particularly with the development of complex weapons of mass destruction. Arms races were not unknown in the ancient world, but there were few instances of organized attempts at negotiations toward the limitation of armaments. In the sixth century B.C., the Hwang Ho states concluded a disarmament treaty with one of the states of the Yangtze Valley, which kept the peace between these countries for a hundred years.[1] Organized international disarmament conferences, however, may be said to have begun with the Hague conferences of 1899 and 1907.

The first Hague conference met from May 18 to July 29, 1899, and was attended by twenty-six nations, including four Asian (Japan, China, Persia, and Siam) and two American (United States and Mexico) states. The conference established three committees to deal with the three major topics:

1. The limitation of armaments and war budgets

2. The extension of the Geneva Red Cross rules of 1864 and 1866 to naval warfare

3. Mediation, arbitration, and other methods of preventing armed conflicts.

The only positive result that emerged from the conference was the establishment of the Hague Court of Arbitration. Even so, none of the participants was prepared to make the court's jurisdiction binding on itself and considered that the court should confine itself to minor cases, such as claims for monetary compensation. It was assumed that the court would not be concerned with the arbitration of political disputes. In short, this first conference contributed very little toward the solution of the problem of disarmament.

The second Hague conference (June 15 to October 18, 1907) was attended by forty-eight states. At the opening session, the British delegate suggested confirmation of the resolution adopted by the previous conference in 1899 regarding the limitation of military expenditures. This suggestion was unanimously accepted, and a resolution was passed that affirmed the desirability of resuming the serious examination of the limitation of military expenditures.[2]

Even though the Hague conferences' contributions to disarmament were minimal, they made significant advances in the revision of the rules of warfare and the prohibition of the use of certain types of weapons. Unfortunately, most of these agreements were violated in subsequent world wars.

THE LEAGUE OF NATIONS

The devastations of World War I and the advances foreseen in weapons technology convinced the nations that arms competition would be disastrous for international peace and security. The Covenant of the League of Nations made disarmament a major preoccupation of the organization, considering it one of the first and principal steps toward peace. Britain and France, the two dominant powers in the League, were gravely concerned about disarmament and the reduction of international tensions; after the rise of Hitler in Germany, the Soviet Union also became a strong advocate of disarmament. Disarmament negotiations under the League were relatively fruitless, however, owing to conflicting national objectives and a lack of trust among the nations.

Interestingly, during this period Soviet disarmament proposals emphasized the idea of control and supervision, whereas the United States insisted that arms-limitation agreements be predicated on the good faith of the participating countries. After World War II, the positions of the two countries were reversed. The United States now holds that no disarmament agreement is possible without adequate provision for inspection, whereas the Soviet Union balks at any idea of inspection, particularly within its national territory.

THE UNITED NATIONS

The U.N. Charter was based on the idea of a concert of five great powers (Britain, China, France, the Soviet Union, and the

United States) that, after World War II, would be jointly responsible
for the maintenance of international peace and security. Disarmament
was thus a minimal concern of the Charter. The congruence of
objectives and ideology among the great powers, upon which concerted
action for peace depended, did not in fact materialize. Instead, an
ideological conflict developed, culminating in the cold war, and con-
tinues to polarize international relations. This situation, together
with the rapid advances that were being made in weapons technology
and particularly in the development and stockpiling of atomic weapons,
suddenly upgraded disarmament as a question of high priority for the
United Nations.

At the Moscow conference of foreign ministers in December,
1945, the foreign ministers of Britain and the Soviet Union had agreed
on the establishment of a commission for the study of atomic energy.
The first session of the U.N. General Assembly, which met in London
on January 24, 1946, also unanimously adopted a resolution that had
emerged from the consultations and subsequent discussions between
Canada, the United Kingdom, and the United States calling for the
establishment of a U.N. Atomic Energy Commission to study and
make recommendations about all phases of atomic-energy development. [3]

The Baruch Plan

At the first meeting of the Atomic Energy Commission on June
14, 1946, the U.S. representative, Bernard Baruch, presented the
following proposals on behalf of the U.S. Government:

1. International control of atomic energy at the source,
   with an authority exercising complete control over
   the production and processing of all raw materials

2. An international licensing system to promote
   peacetime uses of atomic energy

3. The strategic distribution of plants and stockpiles
   of fissionable materials throughout the world

4. Access by the international authority into all countries to conduct inspection and control activities

5. The fixing of penalties for any violations

6. The elimination of the veto power in decisions involving punishment for any violations of the atomic-
   energy agreement.

At the second meeting of the Atomic Energy Commission, on June 19, 1946, the Soviet representative, Andrei Gromyko, submitted a draft convention prohibiting the production of all atomic weapons for the purposes of mass destruction. The Soviet plan envisaged a treaty in which the signatories would agree to destroy, within three months after ratification of the agreement, all atomic weapons and to pass legislation, within six months after ratification of the treaty, providing punishment for violation of the agreement.

The main differences between the Baruch plan and the Soviet proposal concerned the stage at which atomic weapons should be prohibited and international control established; the principle of international ownership and control of all phases of atomic-energy activities, including research; and the application of the principle of unanimity in the Security Council when considering violations of the atomic-energy agreement.

From the Soviet point of view, it made little difference whether the atomic monopoly was held by the United States or whether control was vested in the United Nations or some other agency of a similar composition, since the weighted membership would have ensured the dominance of American views. The Soviet Union considered that in such an organization or authority it would never be able to obtain atomic know-how legitimately, since all legal research would be under the control of the United Nations and thus, in effect, under American control. The Soviet proposal, on the other hand, implied that each nation would be self-policing with regard to compliance with the provisions of the atomic-energy agreement and made atomic-energy development the responsibility of the individual states. This position was unacceptable to the United States, which had called for the gradual disclosure of information, starting with the least-important knowledge and reaching the final stage of elimination of atomic weapons only when an inspection system was in full operation. The positions of the two major atomic powers have been so diametrically opposed that the impasse reached at that time has persisted and has tended to bedevil all subsequent disarmament negotiations.

The problem of inspection and control has been an integral part of the step-by-step approach to disarmament that the United States has consistently insisted upon, being unwilling to jeopardize its national security before a system of international control and inspection had been established. Not surprisingly, the Soviet Union has seen in this position the determination of the Western countries to maintain a monopoly on atomic weapons for an indefinite period. It must, however, be conceded that, if the Soviet Union had accepted the Baruch plan, it would have in effect denied itself the development of a national atomic-energy program. In addition, the Soviet Union saw in Western insistence on inspection a means of conducting espionage on Soviet territory. Yet, it is difficult to see how any meaningful disarmament program can be established without some form of inspection to verify acceptance of the agreement.

Conventional Armaments

On February 13, 1947, the Security Council established a Commission for Conventional Armaments, with the same composition as the Council, charged to formulate general principles and concrete proposals with effective suggestions for the reduction of conventional armaments.

During the first year of the commission's work, progress was slow, and its debates tended to reflect the attitudes of the cold war. This was hardly surprising, since in the existing atmosphere of acute international tension and suspicion it was hardly likely that the protagonists of the cold war would lower their guard or accept each others' professions in good faith. American and Soviet attitudes toward the commission were no different from their attitudes toward the Atomic Energy Commission—ambivalent and unstable, sometimes the two reversing their positions on specific issues.

In 1948, the United Nations called for a census of armaments, but the plan prepared by the French for a census and verification of armed forces was rejected by the Soviet Union on the grounds that it imposed preconditions on the reduction of armaments and failed to make use of the collection of information on atomic weapons.

In January, 1952, the General Assembly established a Disarmament Commission under the Security Council with the mandate to prepare a draft treaty for the regulation, limitation, and balanced reduction of all armed forces and armaments and for the effective international control of atomic energy. The Soviet Union agreed to the formation of the Disarmament Commission, but objected to its mandate being based on the Western position and voted against the resolution to establish the commission. Beginning in 1952, the United Nations had been conducting a series of meetings in an effort to reach agreement on a formula for general and complete disarmament. These meetings were largely fruitless until the Disarmament Commission received treaty plans from both the Soviet Union and the United States. The proposals were similar, each calling for complete conventional and nuclear disarmament in three stages, the establishment of peacekeeping machinery for the disarmed world, and the creation of an international disarmament organization to implement disarmament controls. But, beneath these similarities were radically different approaches to the disarmament process, mainly with regard to inspection and verification, and it is these differences that have hindered progress in this area.

THE PARTIAL NUCLEAR TEST-BAN TREATY

Perhaps the most dramatic achievement of the negotiations between the Soviet Union and the United States on arms control and related problems is the treaty banning nuclear-weapons tests in the atmosphere, outer space, and underwater, which was signed by the two countries on August 5, 1963. However, while the treaty has created considerable lessening of international tension and increased the negotiating rapport between the two major nuclear powers, its contribution to the progress of disarmament is limited. Nuclear stockpiles have not been reduced, nor has the production of nuclear weapons been halted. The programs for underground testing by the two powers remain highly developed, and it appears that the partial ban on nuclear tests has done little to deter the development of ever-more complex and incomparably destructive nuclear weapons.

What the ban has done is to reduce the risk of nuclear pollution, which was becoming a serious problem during the period of unlimited testing. Since the first atomic bomb was detonated, there has been great anxiety throughout the world about the biological and health hazards from nuclear debris. Negotiations for the cessation of nuclear testing were so charged with propaganda and counterattacks, however, that no realistic attempt was made at reaching agreement until the 1960s.

Negotiations for a nuclear test-ban treaty were as difficult and tortuous as the general disarmament negotiations, with both sides looking out more for propaganda advantage than for agreement. Many proposals and counterproposals were made either by Western nations or by the Soviet Union, but there was never enough agreement for concrete steps to be taken. In 1955, the Soviet Union proposed to the Disarmament Subcommittee—established in 1952 and consisting of Britain, the Soviet Union, and the United States—the discontinuance of nuclear tests under the supervision of an international commission. In 1956, the Soviet Union linked this proposal to the dismantling of U.S. foreign military bases. This was clearly unacceptable to the Western powers, which could see little advantage in a test ban that was not part of a larger disarmament agreement.

Predictably, the test-ban negotiations were bogged down on the problem of detection and inspection. The Soviet view was that adequate scientific techniques existed for the detection of all underground tests anywhere in the world and that on-site inspections were therefore unnecessary.

In 1957, the United States proposed a test-ban arrangement linked with the cut-off of the production of all fissionable materials under effective control. Subsequently, the proposal suggested, it would then be possible to eliminate all nuclear testing. Simultaneously, outer space should be restricted to peaceful uses and all nuclear testing in this environment banned. No agreement was possible on either proposal. The debates continued, however.

MORATORIUM ON NUCLEAR TESTS

On June 14, 1957, the Soviet Union proposed a three-year moratorium on nuclear tests under international supervision, monitoring posts being located in Britain, the Soviet Union, and the United States. The United States countered with a ten-month trial suspension of nuclear testing, provided that the Soviet Union would agree to the suspension of the manufacture of nuclear weapons one month after the establishment of an international inspection system. In a departure from its usual stance, the United States proposed that the details of the system be developed during the trial period. The United States was, in effect, proposing that the suspension of tests could become effective before the installation of the control posts. The Soviet reply to the U.S. proposal was that a halt in the production of nuclear weapons would be considered only after the renunciation of their use by the United States. The Soviet Union also considered the ten-month period too short to affect the next series of American nuclear tests. Once again, negotiations on nuclear arms had reached an impasse.

The problem of the feasibility of detecting clandestine underground tests, a major consideration in any comprehensive test-ban treaty, was the subject of intense controversy, particularly among the American scientific community. The number of control posts was also a stumbling block in the way of reaching agreement among the nuclear powers and was never to be resolved.

On March 31, 1958, the Soviet Union announced that it had unilaterally ceased all nuclear testing. If, however, other powers continued to test nuclear weapons, then the Soviet Union reserved the right to "act freely in the question of testing."[4] At the same time, the Soviet Union called on Britain and the United States to halt nuclear testing. In reply, the Western powers suggested a technical conference to study specific control measures for a realistic arms-control program. Again, the United States linked its proposal with a cut-off in the production of fissionable materials for weapons purposes. This was unacceptable to the Soviet Union, and the Americans made a revised proposal for technical talks limited to the detection of nuclear tests.

Seven Western and eight East European scientists met at Geneva from July 1 to August 1, 1958, and, after thirty sessions, agreed on 160 to 170 land-based control posts, 10 ship-based control posts, and also inspection by aircraft. A major technical problem before the scientists was the difficulty of distinguishing between earthquakes and underground tests below one kiloton magnitude. After lengthy negotiations, a five-kiloton threshold was agreed upon.

On August 22, the United States suggested that a conference be convened on October 31 to negotiate the suspension of nuclear-weapons tests and to establish an international control system. The United States indicated that it was prepared to suspend tests on a year-to-year basis coincident on the opening of the conference, provided that progress was made toward the establishment of a control system. The Soviet Union found the U.S. position unacceptable, and the latest impasse between the nuclear powers was dramatized at the opening of the thirteenth General Assembly in September, 1958, when the Soviet Union called for the immediate and unconditional suspension of all nuclear tests, Predictably, the Western powers found this unacceptable.

On October 1, 1958, the Soviet Union announced that it would resume nuclear tests because both the United States and Britain had carried out a major series of tests in the spring and summer and it therefore had the right to resume its own testing until the number of its tests equaled that of the Western powers. Ten days before the conference opened, France also announced that it would not be bound by any test-ban arrangement negotiated by Britain, the Soviet Union, and the United States.

GENEVA CONFERENCE ON CESSATION OF NUCLEAR-WEAPONS TESTS

During the first week of the October 31 conference, the Soviet Union conducted three tests, with the result that the United States felt released from its pledge to forego nuclear tests during the negotiations. The deadlock over a control system was revived during the first month of the negotiations. In the Soviet view, the main objective of the conference was a test-ban treaty; however, it was also agreed to enter into immediate discussion of the control system.

Before the conference adjourned on December 24, the rudiments of a control system had been agreed upon. A seven-nation control commission would have three permanent members—Britain, the Soviet Union, and the United States—and four other members to be elected by the permanent members to serve on a rotating basis. The question of voting procedure still remained a problem. The Soviet Union insisted on the principle of unanimity of the permanent members. The Western powers held that the right of veto on substantive matters would make the commission unworkable, since this would apply to the dispatch of inspection teams by the commission. The composition of the nonpermanent members and the status of the inspection teams were also difficult problems. The Western powers wanted a commission consisting of Britain, the United States, and one ally, plus the Soviet Union, one ally, and two neutrals. The Soviet Union preferred a commission made up of Britain, the United States, and one ally, plus the Soviet Union, two allies, and one neutral. Furthermore, while the Western powers called for permanent inspection teams, the Soviet Union proposed ad hoc inspection teams, to be impaneled when necessary. The nationalities on the inspection teams constituted another problem.

This kind of mutually exclusive negotiating stances characterized most of the negotiations. Meanwhile, the United States had also resumed underground testing and came up with data relating to the difficulties of detecting underground tests. The Soviet Union refused to consider the new technical data. In April, 1959, the United States proposed the suspension of nuclear tests in the atmosphere while the political and technical problems relating to underground and outer-space tests were being resolved. The Soviet Union refused the proposal. This kind of negotiation by counterproposal or rejection continued until November, 1961, when the conference ended without agreement.

EIGHTEEN-NATION DISARMAMENT COMMITTEE

The negotiations were resumed in the Eighteen-Nation Disarmament Committee (ENDC)—composed of Brazil, Burma, Canada, Czechoslovakia, Ethiopia, Hungary, India, Italy, Mexico, Nigeria, Poland, Rumania, Sweden, U.S.S.R., U.A.R., U.K., United States, and France*—which had superseded the Disarmament Commission. The first meeting was set for March 14, 1962, but France withdrew from

---

*The ENDC has been enlarged to twenty-five by the inclusion of Argentina, Bulgaria, Japan, Mongolia, Netherlands, Pakistan, and Yugoslavia.

the committee before that date. The negotiations in this committee were, for obvious reasons, even more charged with propaganda and were no more successful than previous attempts.

On August 1, the United States announced that, on the basis of potential advances in the detection of underground tests, it was prepared to accept national control stations that would be internationally monitored and supervised, but insisted on on-site inspection of all suspicious events. This announcement was followed by modifications regarding the number of control stations and their distribution. The Soviet Union did not accept the modified U.S. position. On August 27, 1962, the Western powers submitted two alternative proposals to the committee. One was a treaty banning all nuclear tests in all environments with internationally supervised, nationally manned control posts and with on-site inspections; the other was a limited ban on nuclear tests in all environments, except underground, and without the need for verification machinery. These proposals received no more acceptance than previous ones. The deadlock continued.

Finally, on June 10, 1963, the United States announced that high-level discussions would begin in Moscow, which, it was hoped, would lead to early agreement on banning nuclear tests. By July 25, a limited test-ban treaty was ready for initialing, and by October 10, 1963, the treaty, prohibiting nuclear-weapons tests or other nuclear explosions in any environment, had come into force. Signatories also agreed not to encourage such testing by other states. The treaty is of unlimited duration, but any party may withdraw after three months' notice if it considers its interests jeopardized.

NUCLEAR NONPROLIFERATION TREATY

As nuclear technology became simplified and the assembling of nuclear weapons came within the capability of many more nations, there was widespread anxiety that the spread of nuclear weapons would pose the greatest risk of nuclear war. By 1960, some eleven states, including the People's Republic of China, India, and Israel, had acquired the technical capability to undertake nuclear-weapons programs.

Concern about the spread of nuclear weapons was based on the fear that it would increase the likelihood of a global nuclear war, since the possession of nuclear weapons by "less-responsible nations" would magnify the potential for accidents or willful use. On the other hand, the nonnuclear nations maintained that unless the curb on further dissemination of nuclear weapons was related to a plan for general disarmament, the existing nuclear monopoly would be made permanent. This position was supported by the French, who were busily developing their nuclear capability.

In the General Assembly, the Disarmament Commission, the ENDC, and in bilateral talks, this concern led to various proposals, which, while widely supported, were in the nature of recommendations; it was not until the late 1960s that a formal treaty was drawn up. On August 17, 1965, the United States submitted a draft treaty to the ENDC, prohibiting the nuclear powers from the following:

1. Transferring nuclear weapons into the national control of any nonnuclear state, either directly or indirectly through a military alliance

2. Taking any other action that would cause an increase in the total number of states and other organizations having independent power to use nuclear weapons

3. Assisting any nonnuclear state in the manufacture of nuclear weapons.

Under the draft treaty, nonnuclear states were to accept the same obligations.

In explaining its draft treaty, the United States stated that a nonproliferation treaty should remain in force indefinitely and should preclude neither possible political developments—particularly in Western Europe—that could result in the establishment of a new political and defense entity, nor the acquisition and control of nuclear weapons by such an entity. When questioned by the Soviet Union about the relevance of the provisions of the draft treaty to the Multilateral Force being considered by the North Atlantic Treaty Organization (NATO) countries, the United States maintained that the proposed NATO nuclear arrangements would not be disseminating and that the United States and its allies would ensure that all future NATO decisions on nuclear arms would comply with the provisions of the treaty. Not surprisingly, the Soviet Union rejected the American draft.

The Soviet argument was that the NATO nuclear arrangements were designed for the sharing of control of nuclear weapons by nonnuclear powers, including the Federal Republic of Germany, and were thus incompatible with a nonproliferation treaty.

At the twentieth General Assembly, in September, 1965, the U.S. draft treaty and a Soviet proposal both came before the First Political Committee. The Soviet draft treaty would:

1.   Prohibit the nuclear powers from transferring nuclear weapons directly or indirectly through groupings of states, into the ownership or disposal of states or groups of states not possessing nuclear weapons, or from granting the aforesaid states the right to participate in the ownership, control, or use of nuclear weapons.

2.   Require powers possessing nuclear weapons not to create, manufacture, or prepare to manufacture nuclear weapons either independently or jointly with other states, and to refuse to be associated with nuclear weapons in any form whatsoever—directly or indirectly— through third states or groupings of states.

After lengthy discussion of the two drafts, the question was referred to the ENDC, with the request for the submission of a nonproliferation treaty at the earliest possible time. On August 24, 1967, the Soviet Union and the United States submitted identical draft treaties on nuclear nonproliferation to the committee. On January 18, 1968, revised identical drafts were placed before the committee. Months of discussion ensued, during which little progress was made. By August, 1968, however, agreement had been reached on the text of a treaty, which was endorsed by the U.S. Senate by an overwhelming vote. The Nonproliferation Treaty came into force on March 5, 1970, prohibiting nuclear powers from transferring nuclear weapons to nonnuclear powers or assisting such powers in developing nuclear-weapons capability. The treaty also enjoins nonnuclear powers from seeking to develop nuclear weapons.

NUCLEAR-FREE ZONES

Treaties have been signed making Antarctica (1959), outer space, the moon, and other celestial bodies (1967) nuclear-free areas. The ensuing discussion concerns attempts to do the same in Central Europe, Africa, and Latin America.

Central Europe

The idea of nuclear-free zones as an aspect of the nonproliferation of nuclear weapons has been discussed in the United Nations and other forums since 1956. The Soviet proposals for disarmament advanced in the Disarmament Subcommittee in 1956 and 1957 included provisions for the banning of nuclear weapons in the armaments of troops stationed on German territory. Subsequently, specific proposals for the denuclearization of Central Europe were presented to the United Nations on October 2, 1957, by the Polish foreign minister, Adam Rapacki. The Rapacki Plan called for the prohibition of the production and stockpiling of nuclear weapons in East Germany, West Germany, Czechoslovakia, and Poland. This plan underwent several modifications to accommodate various objections, and the latest version was presented to the ENDC in Geneva on March 28, 1962. This version enlarged the proposed zone by making the agreement open to any other European country wishing to accede to it. The purpose of the proposal was "to eliminate nuclear weapons and delivery vehicles from Central Europe; and to reduce armed forces and conventional armaments within a limited area in which these measures would help to reduce tension and substantially limit the danger of conflict."[5] The plan was to be implemented in two stages: the first called for a freeze of nuclear-weapons systems and of delivery systems within the zone; the second called for all nuclear-weapons systems to be removed from the zone and conventional armaments reduced, both by the countries whose territory was immediately involved and by those that had stationed armed forces within the area.

The Gomulka proposals, a further variant of the Rapacki Plan, were announced by the First Secretary of the Polish United Workers' Party on February 21, 1964, and submitted to the countries concerned in December, 1963. They were intended to be a partial step toward the realization of the more complicated Rapacki Plan. The main elements of the proposals called for a freeze of the existing nuclear status quo of the four named countries of Central Europe. The governments maintaining armed forces in this area (including West Berlin) were not to produce, import, or transfer to other parties in the area nuclear or thermonuclear weapons. The plan also called for the initiation of an appropriate system of supervision and safeguards.

The Polish proposals were unacceptable to the Western powers because they claimed that nuclear-free zones should form part of an arms-control agreement and should not precede it. The Western attitude was predicated on the contention that the plan could upset the basic principle of balanced disarmament by requiring the Western (mainly American) forces in West Germany to divest themselves of nuclear weapons while leaving the nuclear weapons located in the Soviet Union intact.

Africa

Proposals for the denuclearization of Africa resulted from the French nuclear tests in the Sahara in 1960. In December of that year and in November, 1961, the U.N. General Assembly adopted resolutions sponsored by several African states, calling on member states of the United Nations to refrain from carrying out or continuing to carry out any type of nuclear tests in Africa, to refrain from using the territory or territorial waters or air space of Africa for testing, storing, or transporting nuclear weapons, and to consider the continent of Africa a denuclearized zone.

The United States opposed several clauses of the resolution and abstained in the final vote, its objection being that the resolution would limit the right of self-defense in Africa—a limitation that had not been placed upon states in other parts of the world.

In 1963, the African members of the ENDC submitted to that body a resolution for the denuclearization of Africa adopted in May of that year by the Summit Conference of the Organization of African Unity (OAU). This resolution, which was similar to the previous ones, was subsequently adopted by the General Assembly in December, 1965.

Latin America

During the Cuban missile crisis of October, 1962, Brazil, Bolivia, Chile, and Ecuador sponsored a resolution in the U.N. General Assembly providing for a denuclearized zone in Latin America. The resolution was widely supported, but the General Assembly decided to postpone its discussion until its next session. When the resolution came up for discussion at the next General Assembly, Cuba, while expressing support in principle for the resolution, objected that it failed to provide for the necessary element of security and insisted that the Latin American nuclear-free zone should include Puerto Rico and the Panama Canal Zone and the liquidation of all foreign military bases.

In 1963, a U.N. resolution was adopted that expressed the hope that the Latin American states would initiate studies to determine the measures that should be agreed upon to fulfill the declaration made by Bolivia, Chile, Ecuador, Mexico, and Brazil, indicating their willingness to enter into an agreement prohibiting the manufacture, importation, storage, or testing of nuclear weapons or delivery vehicles. In 1967, a Treaty for the Prohibition of Nuclear Weapons in Latin America was signed in Mexico by several Latin American countries. One year later, the United States expressed its intention to accede to the treaty provided that Puerto Rico and the Virgin Islands be excluded.

THE SALT CONFERENCES

It is not possible, at the time of writing, to make any prognosis of the outcome of the current Strategic Arms Limitation Talks

(SALT) between the United States and the Soviet Union, which are taking place in Vienna. Present indications are that the talks are proceeding as well as might be expected, in spite of the difficulties created for Soviet-American relations by the war in Indochina. This is indicative of the anxiety of both the Soviet Union and the United States to find a way of limiting the development of strategic weapons.

Hopes have been expressed that agreement would be reached during the Vienna talks "to prevent the otherwise inevitable massive deployment of multiple nuclear warheads known as MIRV's" (multiple independently targeted vehicles). [6] The speculation is that the SALT agreement, when achieved, would also embody the freezing, at present levels, of the numbers of rival missiles and would limit the deployment of anti-ballistic missile (ABM) defenses to the protection of Washington and Moscow.

The history of arms-control negotiations indicates that not much progress is possible as long as political differences divide the great powers. It has also indicated the extremely ambivalent postures of the great powers on specific issues. In an atmosphere of intense ideological conflict, hopes for comprehensive disarmament are probably illusory, and one will have to accept the step-by-step approach to partial arrangements for arms control. Disarmament is certainly illusory as long as China is excluded from participating in international affairs.

DISARMAMENT AS AN AFRICAN PROBLEM

In global terms, African defense budgets have not been large enough for the military establishments to constitute a significant international problem. Since the beginning of the 1960s, however, the rise in military expenditures in Africa has been rapid and widespread. The accelerated growth in defense budgets can be related partly to the attempt of the new independent nations to establish their own defense forces and partly to the frantic rearmament of South Africa in the early 1960s.

By and large, the defense expenditures in most African countries have been predicated on the need for the maintenance of internal security, rather than on external military threats. Related to this, an important objective of a majority of African regimes has been the need for establishing a strong basis for their own power through the maintenance of relatively large defense establishments. In some cases, this policy has been counterproductive and has, predictably, led to the ouster of incumbent regimes through coups d'état.

High defense expenditure is sometimes related to the existence
of border problems between African countries. The size of the defense budgets of many African countries is also related to the availability and extent of foreign military aid. Considerations of national
prestige and the defense establishment's own clout in ensuring high
budgetary allocations have also been a factor tending to keep up relatively high defense budgets in some cases.

Even excluding South Africa, the rise in military expenditure
has been spectacular during the past decade—from $258.4 million in
1960 to $703.3 million in 1968 (see Table 1.). The annual percentage
increase has been more than 10 percent (36 percent in 1961-62), with
the exception of 1966-67, when a modest increase of 2.4 percent was
recorded. This compares with a 7-percent average increase for the
developing world as a whole and a 6-percent increase for the developed
countries. The distressing fact is that the annual growth of African
defense expenditures is nearly twice as great as the annual growth
target set by the U.N. Development Decade, which not more than a
handful of African countries have achieved during the decade.

The defense expenditures of fifteen selected African countries
as a percentage of total government expenditures in 1966-67 ranged
from 5 percent to 21 percent—the average being about 11 percent
(see Table 2). While this average is not particularly striking compared to that of countries outside Africa, it becomes very significant
when it is compared to the average expenditure on education, agriculture, or health and shows a relative emphasis on military expenditure in terms of national priorities. This disturbing trend is, re-
grettably, in line with current world trends. In 1966-67, world
military expenditures equaled the total annual income produced by
the 1 billion people living in Latin America, South Asia, and the
Near East. Defense budgets exceeded by 40 percent global expenditures on education by all levels of government and were more than
three times the global expenditures on health. [7]

The solution to the problem of African defense expenditure lies
not so much in disarmament as in arresting the rate of growth in
military expenditures and in drastically freezing the military budgets.
The major preoccupation of African governments should be the search
for ways of making the minimum necessary military expenditures
yield additional payoffs beyond the procurement of guns, tanks, and
aircraft. The army in developing countries can play an important
and constructive role in the process of modernization, and African
countries must devise ways of utilizing their armies beyond the
ceremonial parade and training exercise. The energy of the African
armies, in this period of nation-building, can be directed toward
nonmilitary objectives and thus can make a tremendous contribution
to physical development.

TABLE 1

Military Expenditures in Africa, 1960-68
(million U.S. $)

Year	Total Africa	Total Less South Africa	Percentage Increase	
1960	320.0	258.4	1960-61:	10.3
1961	390.0	292.2	1961-62:	36.3
1962	555.0	389.9	1962-63:	10.3
1963	610.0	449.9	1963-64:	14.8
1964	750.0	517.4	1964-65:	16.5
1965	880.0	602.9	1965-66:	13.2
1966	985.0	682.7	1966-67:	2.4
1967	1,000.0	699.4	1967-68:	14.8
1968	1,100.0	703.3		

Source: Stockholm International Peace Research Institute Yearbook of World Armaments and Disarmament, 1968/69 (New York: Humanities Press, 1970).

But this presupposes either that the army in each case accepts its role in the society as subordinate to the civilian authority or that it has such an enlightened conception of its role in a developing nation as to enable it to make specific contributions to economic development. In the present situation in many African countries, where the military has developed political power coequal to other authorities in the body politic, the idea of a military contribution to economic development might be considered infra dig of military prestige. It is, however, not impossible that the logic of limited budgets and scarcity of skilled labor may make inevitable some military participation in the construction of the national economy.

WORLD DISARMAMENT AND AFRICA

A conventional illusion among most developing countries is the hope that if by some miracle general and complete disarmament should come about, vast resources would be released for aiding world development. This is as much a myth as the wishful thought that the developed nations would earmark 1 percent of their gross national product (GNP) for international development. There are no firm indications that the release of such resources would even lead

TABLE 2

Defense Expenditure As Percentage of Total
Governmental Expenditure, 1966 and 1967

Country	1966	1967
Cameroon	16.0	16.0
Congo (Kinshasa)	21.4	16.3
Ethiopia	20.3	21.0
Ghana	9.3	11.7
Guinea	11.1	8.8
Ivory Coast	5.6	6.3
Kenya	5.1	6.3
Morocco	16.1	11.2
Nigeria	12.0	10.9
Somalia	18.2	19.7
Sudan	13.5	13.7
Tanzania	5.1	7.1
Tunisia	5.2	5.2
Uganda	11.5	9.4
Zambia	7.0	6.0
Average Africa	11.8	11.3

Source: Derived from AID Economic Data Book (Washington,
D.C.: Agency for International Development, December, 1968).

to the diversion of these resources toward socially oriented
development in some of the disarming countries. In any event, these
countries themselves face serious and escalating domestic problems
that would have first call on any freed resources resulting from disarmament.

African countries would thus be well advised to explore ways
of mobilizing their own resources, preferably on a regional basis,
for the development of the continent. Foreign aid, with or without
disarmament, will not be a crucial factor in African development.
Development cannot be achieved by proxy. It will come only as a
result of the sacrifices, sweat, and tears of the Africans themselves.
What assistance that is proffered will, of course, be a welcome
addition; but the major effort must be by Africans in Africa for Africa.

NOTES

1. William F. Ansberry, Arms Control and Disarmament (Berkeley, Cal.: McCutchan Publishing Corp., 1969), p. 20.

2. Ibid.

3. United Nations, The United Nations and Disarmament (New York, 1945-65), p. 13.

4. Department of State Bulletin, XXVIII, 982 (April 21, 1958).

5. The United Nations and Disarmament, p. 210.

6. Washington Post, June 10, 1970, p. 1.

7. World Military Expenditures, 1966-67, Research Report 68-52 (Washington, D.C.: U.S. Arms Control and Disarmament Agency, December, 1968).

NOTES
ON DISARMAMENT
AND AFRICAN
DEVELOPMENT
David Carney

The bearing of disarmament on African development can be examined from two perspectives: the possible consequences of reduced armament expenditures by African countries themselves and the possible consequences of such reduction by industrialized countries, especially the United States and the Soviet Union. The general presumption in both cases is that African development should profit from a reduction in both domestic and foreign armament expenditures.

It is, of course, one thing to argue in favor of diverting arms expenditures into national development, but it is quite another to confidently expect such a diversion to occur as a direct result of a reduction. This chapter accepts that diversion of expenditures for this purpose is highly desirable, but raises doubt about development's being the, or a, principal beneficiary of reduced arms spending.

First of all, one must examine the various causes of rising armament expenditures in African countries. These are many and include the following:

     1. Inability of civilian governments to improve economic conditions in their respective countries—many military coups (e.g., in Haute Volta, Togo, Dahomey) were due to this factor; thus, lack of economic progress can lead to more, not less, military expenditure, and less, not more, economic expenditure.

     2. Inability of civilian governments to maintain order and/or unwillingness to tolerate democratic procedures—an important element in the military takeovers in the Congo (Kinshasa),* Nigeria, and Sierra Leone.

important element in the military takeovers in the Congo (Kinshasa),*
Nigeria, and Sierra Leone.

3.   Relation of a country to the defense perimeter of a great
power. For a long time in the early 1950s, North Africa was regarded
as an essential element in the defense perimeter of the United States—
hence, the establishment of American bases in, and supply of arms to,
that area. With a change in the "balance of terror" and with progress
in military technology, the value of North Africa in the defense
strategy of the United States has declined, while it has increased in
that of the Soviet Union and France. One external source of arms is
being replaced by another.

4.   Countries that are established defense perimeters of major
powers will continue to attract armaments and expenditures on them
(e.g., Egypt and Israel), irrespective of their wishes in the matter,
since they can also become convenient testing grounds for new
weapons.

5.   Mistrust among powers big and small—the basic cause of
armaments spending.

Thus, there are powerful factors, internal as well as external,
accounting for the rise in military expenditures in Africa, as elsewhere. And it would be naïve to think that less arms spending will
automatically or necessarily lead to more development spending.
Furthermore, one must distinguish between growth expenditures and
development expenditures in order to assess properly the significance
of the argument for diverting expenditures from arms to development.
If, for brevity, one defines "development" as "spontaneous and continuing change," and "capacity for development" therefore as "capacity for spontaneous and continuing change," it becomes clear that
there is no inevitable or necessary inverse relationship between arms
expenditures and development. On the contrary, it can be shown that
both capacity for spontaneous and continuing change and military expenditures tend to move in the same direction.

One must regretfully quash the simplistic notion that the bottleneck to African development is on the expenditure side. That little

_____

*Now called Zaire; however, at the time of writing the country
was known as Congo (Kinshasa).

effort and investment have been devoted to change is owing not to an absolute or even relative lack of funds, but to a general lack of awareness of the prerequisities for development—basically, a change in attitude, a switch from nonchange to change-oriented thinking (as opposed to speaking). Given this switch, its reflection on government expenditures will appear mostly in a change in expenditure patterns, rather than in global amounts.

Examination of the recent trends in defense expenditures of certain selected African and other countries—selected in the sense of availability of data, not in the sense of deliberate choice—shows no correlation between the trend and proportions of military expenditures and those of economic or development expenditures (see Table 3). Therefore, there is no firm basis for the notion that less arms spending by African countries will automatically lead to more development spending. Of the countries listed in Table 3, only the following spend approximately 10 percent or more each year on defense: South Africa, Sudan, Tanzania, Togo, U.A.R., Israel, Canada, U.K., United States, and U.S.S.R. Note that these include undeveloped as well as highly industrialized countries.

With the exception of the U.A.R. and Canada, the countries in Table 3 devote approximately one third or more of government expenditures to the purchase of current goods and services, and, with the exception of Kenya, Rhodesia, and Canada, they spend some 10 to 12 percent or more on capital formation. Thus, one can say with certainty of the following countries that they spend 10 percent or more on defense, 30 to 33 percent or more on current goods and services, and 10 to 12 percent or more on capital formation: South Africa, Sudan, Tanzania, Togo, Israel, U.K., United States, and U.S.S.R.

As long as there are some African countries that maintain as good a record as the developed countries in military spending, there is little reason to believe that a reduction in this area by the latter would contribute to economic progress in the former. This is true regardless of the excuses given by African countries for such military spending. For example, Sudan and South Africa may advance the argument of internal security; or Sudan, Tanzania, and the U.A.R. may give reasons based on external security or the liberation of colonial strongholds still remaining in Africa. Thus, where domestic or external security continue to be threatened, there would in any case be a low priority on development, even with the aid of additional funds.

Accordingly, it becomes clear that the main argument for reduction in arms expenditures has to be based on the prior establishment of conditions of peace and security, both internal and external.

TABLE 3

Range of Variation in Percentage of Total Government Expenditures
on Goods and Services, Capital Formation, and Defense, Selected
Countries

Country	Expenditures on Goods and Services	Gross Fixed Capital Formation	National Defense
Ghana, 1962-68	34.3 - 40.3	12.8 - 29.7	6.6 - 11.2
Kenya, 1962-68	44.5 - 52.6	4.8 - 12.3	0.3 - 6.9
Liberia, 1964-67	48.0 - 64.6	15.5 - 33.5[a]	4.5 - 6.5
Malawi, 1962-66	46.8 - 54.3	13.5 - 27.0	2.2 - 2.4
Nigeria, 1962-64	39.1 - 44.6	20.6 - 28.8	8.0 - 11.0
Nigeria, 1962-64	41.0 - 42.9	23.7 - 26.0	3.9 - 6.1
Rhodesia, 1962-68	34.9 - 53.4	5.8 - 19.9	4.8 - 7.3
South Africa, 1963-69	54.9 - 62.9	24.1 - 32.5[b]	10.4 - 14.1
Sudan, 1963-68	30.8 - 43.7	20.7 - 40.5[c]	8.8 - 20.8
Tanzania, 1963-69	n.a.	n.a.	14.3 - 17.6
Togo, 1963-68	65.9 - 79.9	9.2 - 20.1	5.1 - 13.5
Uganda, 1963-68	67.2 - 86.5[d]	13.5 - 32.8[e]	1.6 - 9.9
U.A.R., 1963-68	14.1 - 79.1	20.9 - 85.9[c]	21.5 - 25.0
Zambia, 1962-65	49.1 - 60.2	14.5 - 19.5	3.2 - 14.1
Israel, 1965-69	46.9 - 60.6	18.5 - 27.1[c]	24.0 - 25.8
Canada, 1962-67	13.4 - 18.0	3.7 - 5.0	16.6 - 22.6
U.K. (public sector), 1962-67	40.3 - 43.6	17.7 - 20.7	13.7 - 16.8
United States (federal government), 1965-70	n.a.	n.a.	41.8 - 45.0
U.S.S.R., 1962-68	n.a.	n.a.	12.6 - 16.0

[a]Gross capital formation.
[b]Capital expenditure.
[c]Development expenditure (or budget).
[d]Recurrent expenditure.
[e]Nonrecurrent expenditure.

Source: United Nations, Statistical Yearbook, 1968 (New York), Table 199: Budget Accounts and Public Debt (figures relate to actual expenditures or to estimates).

But this in turn depends on several factors, including relaxation of tensions among the big powers and control of the international traffic in arms by the leading arms-producing countries.[1] As long as arms can be purchased freely on the international market, there is nothing to stop an underdeveloped country from diverting development funds to the purchase of arms for any purpose, whether it be in support of a corrupt regime, civil conflict, or external aggression. It then becomes hypocritical to criticize expenditures by big powers on space exploration while hunger, illiteracy, and want prevail among two thirds of the population of the world! The underdeveloped world does not have a monopoly on the hungry, the illiterate, and the diseased. Indeed, as the level of living rises in the developed countries, dissatisfaction increases among the poor and disadvantaged of their population.

This is one reason why a bit of skepticism may be in order here. Even if the developed countries were to reduce their expenditures on armaments, there are other areas that would demand their immediate attention: food and nutrition, housing, education, slum clearance, and urban development for their disadvantaged. Thus, they may be expected to give first consideration to their own domestic and social problems, rather than to the similar demands of the world's underdeveloped countries.

Another important reason for sober consideration lies in the relationship between capital (development) and recurrent expenditures. As is well known, every unit of development expenditure generates a certain amount of recurrent expenditure, the multiplier effect depending on the nature of the development expenditure. The division between recurrent and capital expenditure, on the aggregate, is normally one in which recurrent expenditure is much greater than capital expenditure.

A proper analysis of the situation would involve a comparison of the marginal changes in capital and recurrent expenditure, in order to determine the incremental recurrent expenditure generated by an increment in capital expenditure. For want of refined data, one may use figures of total instead of marginal expenditure. An example is a summary of the functional analysis of the combined Nigerian federal and regional government expenditures in the period 1960-61 through 1963-64 (see Table 4).

Capital expenditure on general services ranges from one quarter to one half of the recurrent expenses on this same heading; capital to recurrent expenditure on social and community services maintains a ratio of about 1:2 or a little less, while the ratio for economic services is approximately 2:1. Over-all, the ratio of capital to recurrent expenditure is about 2:3.

TABLE 4

Nigerian Federal and Regional Government Expenditures
(in thousand pounds)

Expenditure	Current				Capital			
	1960-1	1961-2	1962-3	1963-4	1960-1	1961-2	1962-3	1963-4
General services	28,581	28,233	29,793	33,899	6,263	7,860	11,969	16,121
Social and community services	36,323	37,769	39,778	35,744	14,795	16,391	15,171	13,135
Economic services	14,464	15,040	14,461	15,179	32,857	35,034	28,957	27,066
Unallocated expenditures	11,316	15,993	19,449	18,207	11,130	7,828	7,832	22,972
Total	90,684	97,035	103,481	103,029	65,045	67,113	63,929	79,294

Source: Annual Abstract of Statistics, Nigeria, 1967, Table 11.6

28

If one were to assume that the aggregate and incremental distribution of capital and recurrent expenditure were the same, then one would be entitled to expect that any diversion of arms expenditures to other uses (development objectives) would result in a similar distribution of the diverted expenditures between capital and recurrent expenses. Thus, even under the best assumptions, capital expenditures on development will not amount to the total value of the diverted expenditures. And insofar as development depends mostly on human resources, much more will be devoted to recurrent than to capital expenditures. Furthermore, there are so many underdeveloped countries that expenditures diverted to them from armaments in the developed countries would make very little difference to the existing situation.

The whole point of this illustration is that the net development effect of any funds diverted from armaments is likely to be less than expected, taking into account the number of needy claimants and the recurrent expenses of development. One related issue here is that the administrative framework for development is very weak in many underdeveloped countries. This would have to be strengthened for effective development to take place. In other cases, e.g., Nigeria or India, the cost of setting up a dozen or more state governments may be so great as to prohibit development spending.

One of the well-known paradoxes of expenditure on armaments is its stimulating effect on technological innovation. This is important in two respects: first, the practical orientation of military research and development provides a possibility of utilizing research results that would otherwise remain in the purely theoretical or speculative realm, and, second, innovations deriving from military expenditures can be applied to civilian uses, e.g., the supersonic commercial air transport or radar. This is not to argue that use-oriented scientific research and development cannot be carried out other than by military research. It is merely to recognize that the normal civilian necessities of society do not ordinarily provide as strong a stimulus to innovation as research oriented around man's aggressive instincts (war) or his love of adventure (space exploration). To argue thus is to raise the awkward possibility that the pace and quality of technological innovation are likely to suffer without the stimulus of military research and development and that, consequently, even the development of the underdeveloped countries may thereby be adversely affected.

It should be noted here that the hindrance to the development of the underdeveloped countries is a lack of science and technology, not of external funds. Consequently, a reduction in the armament expenditures of the industrialized countries will not benefit the underdeveloped countries unless funds diverted toward the underdeveloped countries are matched by an increased availability of scientific and technological opportunities for the training of personnel from those countries and unless the underdeveloped countries use an increasing part of any funds or aid made available by the industrialized countries in restructuring their educational system in the direction of more science education, experimental laboratories, and technological innovations, as well as technical and vocational training. Even without waiting for funds to be diverted from the armaments race of the industrial giants, the underdeveloped countries could help themselves increasingly by taking a closer look at current expenditures on education and training in order to see whether the pattern of expenditure, as well as the system, could not be improved and made more relevant to their needs. This is not the place to go into a detailed examination of educational systems and expenditures, but the importance of the subject needs to be kept fully in mind in order to keep the relationship between disarmament and development in proper perspective.

Finally, even while acknowledging the desirability of disarmament and a reduction in expenditures on armaments, it must be recognized that, for all the foregoing reasons, there would be little change in the situation of the underdeveloped countries from this factor alone. Hence, it would be well not to hope for too much from this source, but to search for other and more fundamental measures of effecting change in the countries that are in great need of development.

NOTE

1. The desirability and the conditions for arms control have been discussed by many authors. This writer has devoted some thought to the matter in a paper entitled "Social Defense Perspectives in Development Planning with Special Reference to Africa, " International Review of Criminal Policy, No. 25 (United Nations, 1967).

3

REGIONAL DEVELOPMENT AND REGIONAL DISARMAMENT: SOME AFRICAN PERSPECTIVES

A. G. G. Gingyera-Pincywa
Ali A. Mazrui

INTRODUCTION

One way of approaching the question of disarmament and African development is to examine first the rationale for African military expenditures and their effect on economic and social development. While indirect, this approach allows the gains from disarmament to become readily apparent.

Examples are drawn from eight African countries—Kenya, Tanzania, Uganda, Zambia, the Congo (Kinshasa), Ghana, Nigeria, and the Sudan—whose experiences are diverse and yet representative. To put such points as are raised here in their broader perspective, the chapter concludes by examining the connection, on the one hand, between African disarmament and disarmament in general, and, on the other hand, between African development and general disarmament. In this way, it is hoped that the confinement of the discussion to Africa will be more easily understood for what it really is: a small segment from a large fruit, other portions of which are as capable of being separated as that represented here.

There are three broad arenas from which the urge for African states to seek arms or military establishments might arise: the outside or non-African world, the African world, and the internal domestic world of each African state.

With the exception of the Arab North African countries, independent African states have been fortunate, since attaining independence, in one significant respect: the lack of desire by outside non-African states to infringe on their independence militarily or through physical force. Such cases of military or physical incursion as have taken place to date have emanated from private or nonstate elements (private incursions) or, technically speaking, on the invitation of those Africans claiming the legitimate right to rule and hence to invite outside assistance (official intervention). Examples of private incursions include the whole phenomenon of white mercenaries serving in such African internal disturbances as those of the Congo and Nigeria during its civil war. Examples of official interventions, on the other hand, are the U.N. involvement in the then Congo on Patrice Lumumba's invitation in 1960 and the American-Belgian paratroop drop on Stanleyville in 1965 at the "invitation" of Moise Tshombe.

On the whole, however, independent Africa has been permitted to enjoy relative security from external military interference. This is particularly fortunate in view of the flimsiness or permeability of African state boundaries, politically and militarily. The power difference between the African states and external powers, as shall be shown, is so adverse against the African states that any invasion by outside forces, especially from the more developed European and North American states, would be easy. As a matter of fact, it is doubtful if any black African state south of the Sahara seriously targets its military establishments at the outside world.

Helpless as they are in this respect, however, the African states have not gone down on their knees before those more powerful than they. If anything, the record of African dealings with such states has ranged from dignified self-assertion in international affairs to intransigence even in the face of external military affront. The latter was expressed by Dr. Obote of Uganda, following the violation of Uganda's frontiers by Congolese fighter planes backed by U.S. assistance: "We blame the government of the United States . . . We have been attacked without provocation on our part . . . We must all be prepared to throw sand, and sacks of sand, in the eyes of the mighty." Dignified self-assertion and dignified death in self-defense then represent the maximum the African states are prepared to do militarily against an outside military threat.

Turning to the situation within the African world itself, there are two reasons that have been recognized by black African states for the maintenance of military establishments: first, the challenge of racist and colonial southern Africa, and, second, what might be termed the failure of Pan-Africanism.

THE CHALLENGE OF SOUTHERN AFRICA

There are three basic elements in the attitude of the majority of black African states toward southern Africa, and all have

militaristic implications, which in turn have expenditure implications. *
The first underlies the OAU support for the liberation movement in
southern Africa—an outgrowth of the realization that white power in
the Republic of South Africa will not abandon its privilege without a
violent challenge, that Britain will not snatch away the reins of power
from the white settlers of Rhodesia, and, finally, that decadent and
foolhardy Portugal will cling to colonial power in Angola and Mozambique unless its hold over these countries is forcibly removed.

The most plausible method at the moment to challenge southern
Africa is the guerrilla warfare being carried out by freedom fighters
in the affected areas. An OAU committee was set up in 1963 to
coordinate their efforts and to encourage unity among them. Another
of the committee's functions has been to try to give international
recognition to the struggle and to generate international diplomatic
and material support. Finally, the committee serves as a funnel
through which funds from the supporting African states can be transmitted to the freedom fighters. [1]

But southern Africa is not a dormant target waiting to be attacked
and to defend itself against the freedom fighters. It poses challenges
of its own beyond its borders—challenges that form another important
rationale for military expenditures in the neighboring independent
African states, especially Zambia and Tanzania. The propinquity of
the southern Africa danger must be a strong explanation for the fact
that Zambia and three nearby states of eastern Africa—Tanzania,
Kenya, and Uganda—are the only regular contributors to the budget
of the OAU liberation committee. It must also account for the additional military expenditures from these states. As one student of the
problem has described it:

> The regional arms race (between southern Africa and free
> Africa) is . . . leading to a diversion of Zambia's and
> Tanzania's resources away from development and towards
> more sophisticated deterrents. Zambia is buying a £6
> million Rapier ground-to-air missile system from Britain,
> which will be operational in 1970 to deter border incursions
> by Rhodesian and Portuguese planes; it is the largest ever
> single military purchase by a black African state. [2]

---

*This does not refer to such black or enclave African states as
Botswana, Lesotho, Swaziland, and Malawi, whose attitude toward
southern Africa is that of reconciliation or collaboration.

The need for deterrence against possible attacks from southern Africa, then, is the second element in the African attitude toward southern Africa.

The third element, while far less obvious, is nevertheless deserving of mention in any examination of the rationale behind military expenditures in Africa: the possibility of a war, not just between southern Africa and guerrillas, but between southern Africa and guerrillas joined in field action by the African states. Brigadier A. A. Afrifa, of Ghana, describes how close the Ghanaian army came to being sent to fight in Rhodesia toward the final days of Kwame Nkrumah's presidency. Knowing Nkrumah's great passion in Pan-African matters, it is easy to give Brigadier Afrifa the benefit of the doubt and hence to accept the veracity of his information. [3]

More recently, and again from as far afield as West Africa, a similar idea indicative of this latent urge to solve the southern Africa problem through a direct military confrontation was heard—this time from Nigeria. One consequence of the Nigerian civil war was to boost beyond imagination the size of the Nigerian armed forces. From a pre-civil war figure of 10,000, it rocketed to 200,000 by the time the war ended. Such a large contingent of armed men was all right as long as the war continued, but with the termination of the war came the inevitable question of what to do with it. General Yakubu Gowan has since been on record to the effect that these forces will not be used (as the rumor then going around had it) to fight for the Rhodesians, who must exert their own efforts. Nevertheless, it is hardly surprising that the reaction should have come as an answer to the suggestion that the overgrown Nigerian army be made use of in solving the problem of southern Africa. Whoever first ventured the hint touched on a feeling shared, albeit largely quietly for the moment, by an African leader. Thus, it must not be discounted offhand from any catalogue of reasons for military expenditures among countries of black Africa, especially the more radical ones.

THE FAILURE OF PAN-AFRICANISM

As to the second reason for the rise in military expenditures—the failure of Pan-Africanism—only two aspects of this complex phenomenon are relevant here for this discussion. Its development will be examined from 1957, the year Ghana gained its independence and proceeded to emphasize one hope of Pan-Africanism—African unity. In the forefront in this campaign was Kwame Nkrumah. As is now well known, however, his strategy of a continental union government turned out to be unacceptable to many—in fact, to the majority—of the African states that subsequently achieved their own independence. These considered his strategy to be too fast and impractical and preferred a gradualist or regionalist approach to African unity.[4] Where the merit in this debate lay is far less important to the discussion here than the fact that no continental union government, based on either strategy, has yet been set up. Even leaving aside the goal of union government, there is yet another sense in which Pan-Africanism may be said to have failed. With the egocentric demands of many independent states, the unanimity of purpose that was characteristic of preindependence African nationalism is breaking down. Steadily but surely receding into the realm of oblivion or of emptiness are such one-time phrases of unity as "African brotherhood," "African solidarity," and other similar Pan-African slogans.

These twin failures of Pan-Africanism have, or have had, military implications. The problems of a decentralized state system without an overarching government, of which modern Europe has had so plentiful an experience since the sixteenth century—namely, interstate suspicion, conflict, war, and hence the necessity for military establishments—have as a result begun to appear unavoidable in the similar state system of Africa. It should hardly be surprising, therefore, that Kenya and Somali should be involved in a border conflict or Uganda and the Congo (Kinshasa) in a shooting fray in 1965 toward the end of the Congolese rebellion of 1964-65. The estrangement, accompanied by mutual threats of military measures, between the two Congos is yet another symptom of the conflict potential of Africa's state system in the failure of Pan-Africanism to make good its promises.

One of the clearest statements of the importance of this factor as a rationale for military expenditures was given by Uganda's foreign minister in a speech, relevantly titled "Geography as a Determinant of Uganda's Foreign Policy," delivered to students of Makerere University. It was Mr. Odaka's contention that Uganda's contiguity with some states that were less than stable made it imperative for that country to develop a large and effective military force. Being landlocked, Uganda sometimes experienced the overflow of violence from the Congo and the Sudan.

What all the above indicate is that, in the absence of overall moderation or of a strong and reliable sense of brotherhood (both of which Pan-Africanism had once promised), African states have to fend for themselves individually for their security and defense in the event of disagreement among themselves.

INTERNAL DISORDER

The paramountcy of the civil police in the maintenance of domestic law and order has by now attained worldwide acceptance.

But the extent to which they will be permitted to exercise this power
may vary from one political system to another, one of the critical
determining factors being the political culture of a state. Specifically,
a political culture characterized by a high degree of dissension among
social groups will tend to resort to the military, rather than to the
police, more often than one in which a modicum of basic agreement
over important issues exists. The United States, with its recurrent
dissension over race, thus tends to make use of its National Guard
more often than, say, Britain, which has no similar major cleavage.

Following this line of argument, all the African states have the
kinds of internal cleavages for which the military, rather than the
civil police, will be required. The commonest and potentially most
explosive of these—what is called the retribalization of politics[5]—
concerns the resurgence of ethnic loyalties in situations of rivalry
for resource allocation and domestic power.

Since independence, there has definitely been a decline of that
phenomenon referred to as "African nationalism," which had found
sustenance in a particular type of colonial situation and was designed
primarily to loosen the controls of alien power. The imperial with-
drawal meant not an immediate end to those emotions, but rather a
gradual decline of their influence on everyday political behavior.

What ought to be noted is that the decline of African nationalism
in many of these countries has also meant the decline of national
politics. Those parties that captured the wave of nationalistic agitation
have in many cases now lost their cohesion and sense of purpose and
thus their capacity to promote a sense of national involvement. In
addition, the decline of political competition and suppression of
political rivals has curtailed the openness of debate and public wooing
for support, on which politics as an activity must inevitably thrive.
In some cases, corruption and electoral malpractices have created
widespread political cynicism among the populace, making it harder
than ever to achieve a sense of national involvement. It is true of
many African states that the golden age of modern politics coincided
with the golden age of nationalism, and when the latter declined as a
major determinant of political behavior modern politics declined as
a nationalized phenomenon. Be that as it may, it was not merely the
boundaries of political activity that were redefined by the rise and
then decline of nationalism, but those of political loyalties as well.

The most direct redefinition of loyalties that took place concerned
the relative strength of ethnic or tribal loyalties on one side and
broader national loyalties on the other. There was often an assumption
among analysts of the African colonial scene that nationalism made
its recruits from the ranks of the detribalized. From these ranks

came the leaders of the anticolonial agitation. And these agitators
were the first distinct and definable class of politicians modern Africa
produced. The politicians were, in the majority of cases, Westernized
or semi-Westernized; it is partly this factor that tended to distinguish
them in the eyes of the spectator as a detribalized group.

This language of analysis, however, did not adequately differentiate between tribalism as a way of life and tribalism as loyalty to an
ethnic group. There were, in fact, two senses of membership of a
tribe: one, the sense of belonging; the other, the sense of participating.
Belonging meant only that one's ethnic affiliation was to that tribe,
but participating implied a cultural affiliation as well, a sharing of
the particular tribal way of life. When analysts talked about detribalization, they often meant a weakening of cultural affiliation, though
not necessarily of ethnic loyalty. One could adopt an entirely Western
way of life but still retain great love and loyalty to the ethnic group
from which he sprang.

An alternative formulation of this distinction is to differentiate
tribalism from traditionalism. African nationalism made its leading
recruits from the ranks of the detraditionalized, rather than the
detribalized. The educated and semieducated Africans who captured
leading roles in the anticolonial movement had indeed lost some
aspects of traditional modes of behavior and adopted others under
the influence of Western education and control. But the erosion of
traditionality did not necessarily mean the diminution of ethnicity.
Among the most radically detraditionalized must be included African
academics at universities, but even before the Nigerian coup of
January, 1966, the universities of Ibadan and Lagos were already
feeling the internal tensions of conflicting ethnic loyalties.

The University College, Nairobi, has at times experienced
comparable difficulties. The Luos as an ethnic group have produced
more scholars in East African than any other single community, and
this despite the fact that it is no larger than many other ethnic groups.
No sociological or sociopsychological study has yet been undertaken
to explain this phenomenon. Perhaps it is too early to see such
significance in it, as the sample of East African scholars is still
rather limited. But the simple fact that the Luos outnumber all other
ethnic groups at the University College has been the cause of some
tension. The situation is not as acute as it must have been at the
University of Ibadan before the first Nigerian coup, when there was
a disproportionate Ibo presence in most categories of staff. But
there is no doubt that at Nairobi, as was the case at Ibadan, even
the most highly detraditionalized of all Africans, the scholars, have
been feeling the commanding pull of ethnic loyalties.

If one insists on looking at the previous colonial phenomenon of agitators as an outgrowth of partial detribalization, one must look at some of the events following independence in Africa as illustrations of partial retribalization. In Nigeria, the latter phenomenon attained tragic dimensions. The Ibos, for so long part of the vanguard of African nationalism, found themselves retreating into an ideology of the paramountcy of ethnic interests. Their deepest political passions were now retribalized. The painful drama of conflict and civil war in Nigeria began to unfold.

In less stark terms, retribalization is also discernible in other parts of Africa. In Kenya, Luo ethnicity has probably significantly deepened since independence, partly in defensive reaction to some government policies. The political passions of several Luo freedom fighters in the colonial struggle have now become to some extent denationalized. The retreat of African nationalism has helped rekindle some primordial flame. In Uganda, three major attempts to secede had to be overcome in recent years: first, Buganda's attempt to go it alone in 1960, when it abortively declared its independence of the rest of Uganda; second, Buganda's attempt in 1966 to drive out the central government from Kampala, which is in Buganda; and, third, the Rwenzururu movement of western Uganda, which sought to detach the Bakongo not only from Toro district, of which they are a part, but also from the whole of Uganda to form a separate republic with fellow ethnics on the Congolese side.

Other instances of separatism in African countries include the crisis in the Sudanese south, which has continued since 1956, when southern soldiers mutinied against northern Arab officers. And in the Congo, there have been the attempted secession of Katanga under Moise Tshombe and the rebellion in Kasai led by J. Mulele and C. Gbenye in 1964-65.

The likelihood of civil disturbances arising from this kind of situation within individual African states is thus a powerful additional reason for military expenditures. In fact, some of the largest military establishments in black Africa are to be found in countries that have experienced this danger of internal fragmentation: Nigeria, with its 200,000-strong armed force; the Congo (Kinshasa), with its 300,000; and the Sudan, with its 200,000. Uganda and Kenya, though not yet endowed with armies as large as these, have very well-organized and effective military establishments. [6]

MILITARY EXPENDITURES

But what is the level of expenditures entailed in these military establishments? Unfortunately, this is not an easy matter to tackle

with regard to some of these countries. Sources are either meager
or nonexistent, and even where there are annual estimates of expenditures, they are difficult to obtain and often are unusable. The U. N.
Statistical Yearbook, which provides a wide range of statistical data
on diverse countries, was not useful for the purpose, because its
entry for military expenditures is amalgamated and entered as a
single figure with expenditures on general administration. Another
possible source, the Statesman's Yearbook, has figures of the sizes
of the armed forces and types of weapons, but not the magnitude of
expenditures. Even so, the data on the armed forces appear out of
date, while those on weaponry are inadequate for comparative purposes,
as diverse weapons types are catalogued without an effective guide
as to how they compare in cost, size, and effectiveness. Tanzania,
Uganda, and Kenya each publish statistical abstracts, but the first
two countries give no data specifically relevant to military expenditures.

It has thus been necessary to make use of much less direct
sources, one method being to judge the weaponry involved in military
establishments south of the Sahara, an aspect on which a detailed
study was recently completed. The assumption is that the more
sophisticated the weaponry, the higher the level of expenditure involved,
and vice versa.

A recent study along this line is that by John L. Sutton and
Geoffrey Kemp, of the Institute for Strategic Studies in London. [7]
Their paper on arms to developing countries analyzes the distribution
in the developing countries of four major weapons types: aircraft,
guided missiles, warships, and tanks. According to their findings,
it was only South Africa and Rhodesia that had effective and well-
equipped air forces in sub-Saharan Africa. And with regard to warships and tanks, the only country that could be said to possess any
relevant power was South Africa. Some of the other sub-Saharan
countries had armored cars, but, according to the authors, these did
not reflect a significant combat capability toward other states, being
useful principally for maintaining internal security.

Furthermore, Sutton and Kemp discovered that, with the exception of the Caribbean, sub-Saharan Africa had the lowest monetary
value in weapons among the zones of the underdeveloped countries
studied in the analysis. This meagerness with regard to weaponry
is emphasized when a global assessment is made. According to an
article by John H. Haagland, which appeared in the Spring, 1968,
issue of Orbis, six countries—the United States, the Soviet Union,
the United Kingdom, France, West Germany, and Communist China—
"account for about 85 percent of the world's military expenditures;
the remaining countries, about 130 in number, account for only about
15 percent. " As has already been seen, Africa, with the exception
of South Africa and Rhodesia, comprises very little even of this 15
percent.

But how does this slight share by Africa in the world's total military expenditures relate to the production of wealth in the sub-Sahara? A suitable index for use in answering this question would be the ratio of military expenditure to gross domestic product. Here again, in the absence of direct primary statistics, one must depend on secondary material. Tim Shaw gives an index of the ratio of military expenditure to gross domestic product (GDP) for four of the selected countries as follows: Tanzania (0.3), Zambia (2.5), Congo (K) (1.7), and Nigeria (0.9).[8] The best way to appreciate how high a level of military expenditures these percentages represent is to look at them side by side with those pertaining to some other countries. For this purpose, these countries are divided into two groups: Group A, consisting of countries generally known to be militarily active, such as the United States, the United Kingdom, and France; and Group B, or those military inactive, such as Austria, Denmark, and Finland. The figures for Group A, compiled by a team of U.N. economists for the period 1957-59, were 9.8, 6.5, and 6.2, respectively; for Group B, they were 1.5, 2.8, and 1.7, respectively.[9]

It thus becomes clear that percentage-wise the military expenditures of the African states are, as noted earlier, exceptionally moderate.* And it is well that they should be, given the miserably low levels of both their absolute and per capita GDP (see Table 5).

DISARMAMENT AND DEVELOPMENT

Although the level of expenditure is small, it nevertheless represents a diversion of resources from peaceful to military purposes, and, as has been shown, these resources originated from a very small base of GDP. Against this meagerness of wealth produced in African countries, there is the staggering array of development problems, all demanding the application of these limited resources for their solution. Without military expenditures, at least two vital savings could be made and used for civilian projects.

First of these savings is in foreign exchange. All of the eight selected countries, and in fact all countries in Africa, have to buy their weapons from outside, using valuable foreign exchange that could be used to import other goods. Although, as has already been noted, this figure is very low compared with those for the rest of the world, such a foreign-exchange drain from Africa is proportionally serious.

---

*The fact that the indexes of countries in groups A and B, though worked out many years ago, are still higher than the recent ones of the African states adds emphasis to this point.

TABLE 5

Estimates of Total and Per Capita GDP
(million U.S. dollars)

Country	Absolute GDP				Per Capita GDP			
	1958	1963	1966	1967	1958	1963	1966	1967
Kenya	583	852	1,062	1,098	76	96	110	111
Tanzania			792	797			66	67
Uganda	410	493	653	694	64	68	84	87
Zambia	394	578	903	1,052	130	166	236	267
Congo (K)	1,168	1,743	1,542		87	116	96	
Ghana								
Nigeria	2,589	3,931	4,496		52	71	75	
Sudan	915	1,200					196	
United States	412,873	541,100	694,637	732,768	2,361	2,857	3,528	3,680
United Kingdom	56,311	74,983	90,857	93,082	1,090	1,397	1,660	1,690
France	49,843	71,097	91,745	98,940	1,113	1,486	1,857	1,984
Austria								
Denmark								
Finland								

Source: United Nations, Yearbook of National Accounts Statistics, 1968, Vol. I.

A second, more obvious saving is in manpower. Within military establishments is locked manpower that possesses in some respects technical know-how, discipline, and even the work-oriented ethic necessary for development. With the end of World War II, many disbanded army men provided economic and sometimes even political leadership among their people. There is certainly ground for hope that, once converted to civilian tasks, soldiers could significantly contribute to development in their respective countries. Not all the manpower will be immediately absorbed elsewhere; there will be the tensions of adjustment. But economic expansion is not inconsistent with delayed absorption of available labor.

There is a related respect in which military disbandment would contribute positively to African development. While, as has been seen, there are strong reasons for maintaining military establishments, many African countries have not yet solved the problem of what to do with the soldiers during periods of peace. The situation in Nigeria, for example, indicates that, valuable as African soldiers are during crises, they are unproductive and often idle when the threat is over. Of the countries selected, Tanzania has made a move to involve its soldiers in nation-building; Uganda is now experimenting by engaging soldiers in self-help projects, such as the building of their own barracks. Stated simply, disarmament would put to maximum employment people who are now underemployed.

This analysis has been confined to Africa and, specifically, to eight African countries. This must not be misunderstood as taking the position others have taken regarding Africa as a potential laboratory for regional arms-control policies. Lincoln S. Bloomfield and Amelia C. Leiss, for example, once described sub-Saharan Africa as "the outer space of regional arms control, for it is not yet militarized." In an article based on material from a report they prepared under contract with the U. S. Arms Control and Disarmament Agency, the two authors asserted:

> The chances for aborting a regional arms race may be
> greatest in sub-Saharan Africa, where arms levels are
> lowest . . . United States policy could well aim at the
> control or limitation of all arms in both North Africa
> and sub-Saharan Africa . . . [10]

To radical African opinion, this kind of recommendation is in an ominous imperial tradition. Lenin, the architect of modern Russia, once argued that imperialism was "the monopoly stage of capitalism." One of the authors of this chapter has had reason to assert elsewhere that it would be truer to say that imperialism was the monopoly stage of violence. Nor was this intended as a mere

witticism.   Implicit in concepts like that of Pax Britannica was the
idea that the white races had a duty to disarm the rest of mankind.
And so, when the champions of imperial rule were at their most
articulate in its defense, one argument they advanced was that imperialism had given the African, for example, a chance to know what life
was like without violence.   In 1938, Kenyatta could therefore complain
bitterly in the following terms:

> The European prides himself on having done a great serv-
> ice to the Africans by stopping the "tribal warfares," and
> says that the Africans ought to thank the strong power that
> has liberated them from their "constant fear" of being
> attacked by the neighboring war-like tribes.   But consider
> the difference between the method and motive employed in
> the so-called savage tribal warfares and those employed
> in the modern warfare waged by the "civilized" tribes of
> Europe and in which the Africans who have no part in the
> quarrel are forced to defend so-called democracy. [11]

It is to be remembered that this complaint was made about a year
before World War II.   World War I had been enough to demonstrate
the white man's capacity for self-mutilation while still asserting the
right to disarm the colored races, except, of course, for purposes
of fighting the white man's wars.

The Third Pan-African Congress, held in Lisbon in 1923, was
already challenging this doctrine of the white man's exclusive right
to initiate war.   The Congress first argued the link between Negro
dignity and world peace: "In fine, we ask in all the world that black
folk be treated as men.   We can see no other road to peace and progress." It also asserted a connection between Negro dignity and the
right to bear arms, though in a framework that called for general
disarmament.   Implicit in the demands of the congress was that if the
white man was going to insist on disarmament for everyone else, he
must also renounce his own weapons.   And so the Third Pan-African
Congress called for "world disarmament and the abolition of war; but
failing this, and as long as white folk bear arms against black folk,
the right of blacks to bear arms in their own defense."[12]

In each colony the imperial doctrine of monopoly of violence
merged with a more familiar doctrine of political analysis—the idea
that in a political community only the rulers ever have the right to
use violence in dealing with the citizens.   Indeed, political analysts
since Weber have sometimes defined the state in terms of its "monopoly of the legitimate use of physical force within a given territory."[13]
A variant formulation of this same idea in the West is the ethic that
no citizen should "take the law into his own hands." This again is
an assertion of state monopoly in certain forms of coercion.

When the colonial power became, to all intents and purposes, "the state" in many parts of Asia and Africa, a doctrinal merger took place between this principle of state monopoly in physical coercion and the imperial claim of monopoly in warfare and violence. In the total ideology of imperialism and racialism, the right to initiate violence became a prerogative only civilization and statehood could bestow.[14] Black militancy in both Africa and the United States has since challenged this old Caucasian monopoly of the right to initiate violence.

What emerges from this is that regional disarmament within Africa, though attractive in itself, is politically impossible on its own. Economically, regional disarmament would release resources that could be utilized in other sectors of national life. There is also the possibility that when law and order are entrusted to a modernized police force in Africa, and armies as such are abolished, African political stability might not be adversely affected.

But African disarmament without world disarmament would not be an act of moral leadership. It would not avert world crises. It might enhance Africa's developmental capability—but at the cost of reducing in advance its say in global negotiations about the kind of security system mankind as a whole now needs to devise. An Africa already disarmed would be an Africa without credentials for determining the conditions under which others may also be disarmed. It is the old Bevanite problem of "going into a conference chamber naked." In the final analysis, both regional disarmament and regional development require a fundamental reappraisal of the global military and economic systems in their wider ramifications.[15]

NOTES

1. Tim Shaw, "South Africa's Military Capability and the Future of Race Relations," revised version of paper presented at the Conference on Africa in World Affairs, "The Next 30 Years at Makerere," in December, 1969.

2. Ibid.

3. A. A. Afrifa, The Ghana Coup (London: Frank Cass, 1966).

4. See A. Mohiddin, "Nyerere and Nkrumah," paper for U.S.S.C., Makerere, January, 1969; and D. Thiam, The Foreign Policies of African States (London: Phoenix House, 1965), Pt. II.

5. Ali A. Mazrui, "Violent Contiguity and the Politics of Re-Tribalization in Africa," Journal of International Affairs, XXIII, 1 (1969).

6. The Stateman's Yearbook, (London: 1969-70).

7. John L. Sutton and Geoffrey Kemp, Arms to Developing Countries 1945-1965 (London: Institute for Strategic Studies, 1966).

8. T. Shaw, "South Africa's Military Capability."

9. Seymour Melman, ed., Disarmament: Its Politics and Economics (Boston: The American Academy of Arts and Sciences, 1962), pp. 383-96.

10. Lincoln S. Bloomfield and Amelia C. Leiss, "Arms Control and the Developing Countries," World Politics, XVIII, 1 (October, 1965), pp. 6, 7.

11. See Jomo Kenyatta, Facing Mount Kenya (first published in 1938) (London: Secker and Warburg, 1959), p. 212.

12. See George Padmore, ed., History of the Pan African Congress, pp. 22-23.

13. See Max Weber, "Politics as a Vocation," in H. H. Gerth and C. Wright Mills, eds., Max Weber: Essays in Sociology (New York: Oxford University Press, 1958), pp. 77-78.

14. See A. G. G. Gingyera-Pinyewa, "Commonwealth Africa and Black Power in America: Shared Themes in Racial Experience" (unpublished paper). These ideas are discussed in a wider context in Ali A. Mazrui, Towards a Pax Africana (Chicago: University of Chicago Press, 1967), Ch. 12.

15. See "Economic and Social Consequences of Disarmament," in Seymour Melman, Disarmament, p. 332.

It was suggested at the beginning of the session that discussion be conducted along the following lines:

1. Examination of the nature of disarmament negotiations to date
2. Consideration of some of the problems of arms expenditures in Africa
3. The rationale behind large arms budgets and the effects
4. Africa's influence in disarmament negotiations
5. The present role of the army, as compared with its role in the new Africa
6. The influence of the international arms trade on African defense budgets
7. The impact of the situation in South Africa on the military budgets of African countries
8. Africa's position with regard to the recent U.K. decision to sell arms to South Africa and the long-standing French policy of supplying arms to South Africa at great profit
9. Whether disarmament could not only cure some of Africa's ills, but also have a beneficial effect on development
10. The role of nonmilitary personnel in military regimes
11. The effect of public media on security and on the level of arms expenditures.

First Participant: Above and beyond the issue of the effects of disarmament, there were a number of problems confronting Africa as a continent that were so pressing the symposium was duty-bound to discuss them. These included the increase in the rate of arms spending in African countries, the inability of some countries to maintain law and order, and the intervention of the military in political spheres.

Second Participant: Of major interest was whether funds were or were not a limiting factor to African development, or whether progress could have been achieved merely by a reordering of systems and priorities. For example, much money was wasted in providing the wrong kind of education. Certainly, a system that was suitable for less than 50 percent of the people was to be questioned. While most African countries believed that they were aspiring toward a democratic educational system, they had in fact ended with an elitist system.

Third Participant: While it could not force countries to disarm, the symposium could make its views known through various international forums concerned with disarmament negotiations. In this connection, adequate representation of the less-powerful nations on such bodies was essential.

Fourth Participant: "Adequate representation" here was no guarantee that the African countries would have great influence in these councils: much would depend on the caliber of this representation, owing to the often highly technical and complex nature of the discussions.

Fifth Participant: In disarmament negotiations, the big powers failed to give due consideration to the effect of armaments on the rest of the world; furthermore, world public opinion seemed to have little influence on these negotiations. The symposium might consider specific ways in which the rest of the world could make its voice heard.

Sixth Participant: Discussion in depth of disarmament negotiations, while interesting, would be rather fruitless. The two great powers were the only ones who could wage or prevent war, who could negotiate a disarmament agreement, or who could refrain from doing so. It was instructive that in spite of all the lip service paid to the U.N., both Russia and America made no bones about by-passing the U.N. on matters affecting their vital interests. Vietnam, West Berlin, the SALT talks were cases in point. It would prove more useful to examine such issues as the role of the army in African politics, and the southern African situation and its effect, if any, on African military budgets.

Seventh Participant: One of the important things to reflect on was that there were two entirely separate spheres of international activity: one, the strategic or national interest sphere, which was a powerful motivation of governments; the other, the domestic sphere. In most cases, domestic factors were the ultimate consideration in decisions of international affairs. There were times, however, when it was very important to the United States what Africans or Asians or Latins thought. Governments were anxious to avoid international criticism. This was an important factor in the Middle East, where the prestige of great powers was involved. World strategy and regional arms problems, however, were of a different order. While it seemed unlikely that Africans could significantly alter the strategic plans of the great powers, their influence on the arms policies of those powers in Africa could be great. Several factors were involved:

1. The recognition of danger: If the United States, the Soviet Union, or the Africans recognized the danger to themselves of giving or not giving arms, they would obviously be influenced by it.

2. Cost: A few years ago, obsolete equipment could be given away almost gratis; today, arms had to be bought off the production line, and this was expensive, particularly the sophisticated advanced weapons.

3. Domestic pressure: On the American side, there was a real constituency on African affairs, i.e., the 20 million black Americans whose influence, if mobilized, could be powerful.

4. The awareness that most governments appear to want arms: It was clear to both the Soviet Union and the United States that, whatever was said in disarmament conferences, all the African governments were delighted to have new shipments of arms. This factor was solely under the control of Africans.

Fourth Participant: In assessing the influence of public opinion, much depended on whose public opinion one was talking about. In the reaction to the British Government's announcement of its intention to resume arms sales to South Africa, a letter from the Prime Minister of Canada appeared to have carried more weight, judging from the reaction of the British press, than all the recriminatory reactions of the African states.

First Participant: Before embarking on a discussion of the motivation behind arms spending, the symposium might agree on a definition of the role of the army in African states. The traditional definition—that of assisting in the maintenance of internal security and the protection of the territorial integrity of the nation—was as applicable to Africa as to any other part of the world. On this view, military intervention in politics and the maintenance of large military establishments for territorial aggrandizement were both ruled out.

Eighth Participant: It would be unrealistic for an idealist definition of the role of the army: Africa's problems were such that in many countries there were valid reasons for the army's intervention in politics.

Fourth Participant: While military control might be the actuality in some African countries, this could by no means be considered a "normal" state of affairs. In Latin America, for example, the benefits accruing to the people from such "normal" regimes were few.

Ninth Participant: An idealistic definition of the role of the army also assumed certain idealistic qualities of civilian rule—that there existed a system of government that was democratic, honest, and responsive to the needs of the people. This was not the case in many countries, and the army might play a useful role by making sure the politicians did their jobs properly. In this sense, the army could be one of the checks and balances required to make the political order function effectively.

Second Participant: In certain cases, such as the Congo (Kinshasa) and Nigeria, the military regime was necessary not only in preserving order but also in keeping the country together. It might be that in the larger developing countries, the army might be necessary for national integration, for keeping together diverse and paratribal groups.

Sixth Participant: Views making military intervention in politics justifiable on grounds of national integration raised the fundamental question of legitimacy. On what basis could the army presume to be the arbiter of politics? It was naïve to assume that, by accepting the hastily assembled "democratic constitutions" bequeathed by the colonial powers, African countries were, by some miracle, going to be transformed into a collection of "instant" democracies. Democracy in African society would not be possible without the development of other countervailing centers of power besides the monolithic political party or the army.

First Participant: Like others, African states considered that military power could increase their influence in the councils of nations. There was also the feeling that a strong military was an insurance against external attack. These were, however, merely rationalizations, illusory because arming by one state inevitably led to similar action by neighboring states—and an arms race had begun. Internally, large armies had tended to lead to coups d' état.

Second Participant: The deplorable racist policies of South Africa and its belligerent external posture were a threat to peace in southern Africa and a direct factor in the defense policies of African countries such as Zambia and Tanzania. The British argument that the South Africans needed arms to protect the sea routes around the Cape of Good Hope was disingenuous at best. On another level, the speaker wondered whether armed confrontation by the independent African states was the answer to the problem of southern Africa. In certain quarters, it was thought that Malawi might be searching for an alternative approach to the problem of influencing South Africa to modify its racist policies.

First Participant: The potential threat of South Africa and Rhodesia to the independent African states to the north had led to

increasing arms expenditures by Zambia and Tanzania, to the detri-
ment of their economic development. The recent British intention of
resuming arms sales to South Africa could not but aggravate the
situation. In this connection, the African and Asian members of the
Commonwealth felt that they had been betrayed. There was strong
feeling among the African Commonwealth countries that the British
decision was an affront to the concept of a "multiracial Commonwealth"
and that the African states should contract out of the Commonwealth
or—perhaps with tongue in cheek—"drum Britain out of the Commonwealth. "

Tenth Participant: The symposium might consider what courses
of action were open to the African states in the situation of Western
assistance to South Africa.

Sixth Participant: The answer to this question would depend, to
a large extent, on the degree of cohesion within the Organization of
African Unity (OAU) and on the resolution with which the African states
pursued collective policies in convincing all the Western powers that
those who gave aid and succor to South Africa were the enemies of
African freedom and dignity. One way of giving concrete expression
to African determination would be to deny to those countries who
valued dividends from their South African investments more than the
friendship of Africa access to the vast resources of the rest of Africa.
This would require a concerted African policy supported by most of
the African states. It would also entail enormous sacrifices.

Eleventh Participant: Pan-Africanism was not, as was suggested, on the decline; nor was there acceleration of retribalization
in many parts of Africa. The Scientific Council for Africa, by encouraging the development of Pan-Africanist activities in the field
of science, thus fostered scientific cooperation in Africa—clearly
a gain, not a retreat.

Twelfth Participant: Evidence of the Pan-African spirit was
the OAU's offer of material and moral support to the liberation
movements in Africa. And since there was need to support the fight
against the colonialists, arms could not be entirely banned.

Fifth Participant: The division of the continent into such a
bewildering number of states—in spite of many unifying factors—in
itself created problems of communication and cohesion. While
this division might increase Africa's voting strength in the United
Nations, it was bound to have polarizing effects on the political future
of the continent.

Sixth Participant: There was little doubt that Pan-Africanism

II

SCIENCE, TECHNOLOGY, AND DEVELOPMENT

4

SCIENCE
AND TECHNOLOGY
IN DEVELOPMENT:
AN OVERVIEW
Frank G. Torto

The Pugwash conferences began with a meeting in Pugwash in July, 1957. Discussions at this and the meetings that followed at frequent intervals centered on the hazards arising from the use of atomic energy in peace and war, the control of nuclear weapons, and, generally, the role that scientists—especially those involved in atomic research—could play in the preservation of peace. A departure from these subjects was made in 1961, however, at a meeting held in Stowe, Vermont, which had as its main theme "International Cooperation in Pure and Applied Science" and, as a major subdivision on the agenda, "Assistance to Developing Nations and Exchange of Scientists and Scientific Information." Aspects of this theme have figured in most of the conferences since 1961, with the fifteenth conference at Addis Ababa, in 1966, being devoted to "Science in Aid of Developing Countries."

The decade 1960-70 has been marked both by a concern for advancing the development of the so-called developing countries and by an appreciation of the crucial role that science and technology in combination have to play in the process of development. Not only at the Pugwash conferences, but at a number of other international conferences as well, it has been generally agreed that action is needed to speed up the advancement of these countries.

The first really large conference appears to have been the International Conference on Science in the Advancement of New States, held at Rehovot, Israel, in 1960, which was attended by some 120 delegates from 40 countries of Africa, Asia, Europe, North America, and South America, and by representatives of U.N. specialized agencies.

Perhaps the most significant was that held by the U.N. in Geneva, the Conference on the Application of Science and Technology for the

Benefit of the Less Developed Areas, in February, 1963. More than 2,000 papers were submitted, and there were nearly 1,700 participants representing 96 governments and specialized agencies and organizations. Subjects discussed at this conference include those that have engaged the attention of subsequent conferences: natural resources; human resources; agriculture; transport; health and nutrition; social problems of development and urbanization; organization, planning, and programming of economic development; scientific and technological policies; international cooperation; and problems of transfer, adaptation, and training of scientific personnel.

The purpose of this paper is to review the main conclusions that have emerged from the various conferences and meetings insofar as they relate to the advancement of the developing countries.

PLANNING OF SCIENTIFIC AND TECHNOLOGICAL POLICY

Science Advisory Council

It has been advocated that every country should have a central scientific and technological body, such as a scientific advisory council, responsible for the elaboration of a national science policy. Such a policy would include recommendations on national priorities and the allocation of resources to these priorities. There should be close liaison between the advisory council and the government organ responsible for planning national economic and social development, in order that the science policy can promote these objectives and so that the objectives themselves may take into account the possibilities arising from the application of scientific and technological knowledge.

The advisory council should not be attached to any particular government ministry or department, but should have its governmental links with the cabinet through the office of the prime minister or president. The membership of the advisory council should include representatives of relevant government departments and ministries, industry, the universities, research institutes, and learned societies. There should also be practitioners of the social sciences, to ensure attention to the economic and social aspects of the policies. A high proportion of the scientific categories should be practicing scientists. The advisory body should have a reasonable degree of stability and freedom from direct interference, which may be motivated by political considerations, in order that continuity in pursuing policies and projects be maintained.

Types of Scientific Activity

A realistic and balanced combination of different types of scientific activity, appropriate to the resources and needs of the country, will have to be undertaken. In most developing countries, significant advances can be made by the direct application of technologies that have been worked out in other countries. In many cases, there will be the need for adaptive research if the imported technologies are to be successfully applied to local conditions. This form of applied research should be the first line of attack on problems, since any other approach would be a waste of time and resources. In many developing countries, the greatest research need will be in the applied research field, whether it is adaptive or original, and in experimental development, involving pilot plant studies and the building of prototypes.

A certain amount of fundamental research is essential for long-term development. With the scarcity of material and manpower resources, however, fundamental research should, preferably, be "oriented" rather than "pure." Thus would be met the need for gathering basic information about the local environment, such as its climate, geology, and plant and animal life. Fundamental research would also promote the creation of a scientific climate necessary for high-quality endeavor in all fields, including the applied-research field, and foster the healthy development of scientific teaching and research in universities.

Research Agencies

Research would be conducted by a number of agencies. These would include specialized research institutes concentrating on narrow areas, such as soils, forest products, medical research, crop research, and so on, or commodity research institutes devoted to single crops or products, such as cocoa, coffee, or oil palm. Multidisciplinary research institutes, with laboratories and specialists in many related disciplines in the same organization, are believed to offer certain advantages, including the sharing of common services and the ease and convenience with which they can undertake "project research," in which different disciplines are brought to bear on one problem requiring urgent attention. Project research, with definite time schedules, is believed to be one of the most effective weapons for tackling the problems of developing countries.

Much discussion has centered on the relative roles of universities and of research institutes. One extreme view has held that universities should concentrate on teaching and fundamental research and should not get involved in applied research. Another view, strongly supported at the Pugwash conferences, is that, with the scarcity of trained scientific manpower and of physical resources in most developing countries, the universities must be prepared to conduct essential national research, including applied research and, in appropriate cases, experimental development.

Relationships Between National Science Council and Research Agencies

The relationships between the different agencies conducting national research, and, in turn, their relationship to the national scientific advisory council, must be defined. The advisory council may function, as far as implementation of policy is concerned, by serving as a coordinating agency to delegate responsibility among the various research institutes and university departments. It may, on the other hand, be vested with executive powers, involving the control of a number of research institutes that undertake fundamental research, applied research, and development.

The executive functions of the council would include the recruitment, appointment, and discipline of staff, the regulation of conditions of service, and the control of funds. The entire organization should be outside the civil-service structure to ensure flexibility and to insulate institutes from unnecessary bureaucracy, changes in policy, and the diversion of funds, in times of stringency, to other purposes.

With regard to the role that universities should play in national research, the council could award grants and contracts to certain departments for appropriate research programs. There could also be close physical and organic relations between research institutes and universities by the siting of institutions close to or on university campuses and by the participation of the staff of both organizations in joint research and teaching activities.

Whatever the institutional relationships between the agencies conducting research and the national science advisory or research council, it should be the council's concern that, insofar as possible, all research programs are in harmony with the national scientific and technological policy for the economic and social advancement of the country.

INFRASTRUCTURE FOR SCIENCE
AND TECHNOLOGY

Scientific and Technological Manpower

One of the greatest barriers to the rapid advancement of developing countries, through the application of science and technology, is the lack of adequate supplies of trained manpower. The creation or extension of facilities for training such manpower, therefore, deserves priority attention. There should be adaptation of the curriculum and content of syllabuses to reflect the needs of the environment, as well as the latest advances in effective methods of science teaching. The use of audio-visual methods should be exploited in order to relieve the widespread teacher-shortage problem.

In addition, university facilities for training graduates and postgraduate workers should be expanded. The training of workers close to the environment in which they will have to function has advantages over training abroad. This is particularly so if undergraduate courses of instruction and postgraduate research projects are related to the country's problem.

In order to attract persons of high caliber into scientific professions, they must enjoy status and remuneration and have career structures that place them at no disadvantage as compared with those in nonscientific careers.

Supporting Personnel and Auxiliary Services

Attention should be given to facilities for training of supporting technicians of all levels and to the provision of auxiliary services for research. These would include well-equipped workshops for the maintenance, repair, and manufacture of electronic and other equipment, manned by highly qualified personnel.

Libraries and Documentation Centers

With the creation of good libraries, documentation centers, and information services, research workers would be able to study published results that are relevant to their work and thereby avoid wasting time trying to discover knowledge that is already available. It has been argued that since comprehensive documentation centers are very expensive to maintain, their main purpose in developing countries should be to provide information about sources of information. They could also, usefully, be of assistance in obtaining access to such sources. Wherever possible, however, they should develop the full range of services, including abstracting and translation of published material.

Science Administrators

The organization of science itself must be treated seriously and scientific administration placed in the hands of administrators of high caliber and training. Those responsible for planning and execution in this field should study the experience of similar organizations in other countries.

APPLICATION OF RESEARCH RESULTS

The allocation of funds and manpower is necessary if research and experimental development results are to be translated into economically beneficial projects. This could be done by scientific officers in liaison units attached to research institutes, who would organize frequent demonstrations of prototypes and pilot scale experiments to potential users of the processes and products. Special extension units are also required to conduct publicity and education campaigns, in towns and villages, to introduce new products or improved methods of production.

In regard to agricultural extension, it is imperative first that research findings be translated into simple instructions that can be readily adopted by peasant farmers. Then there must be frequent demonstrations, whenever possible on these farms, of new crops, new methods, improved management practices, fertilizers, insecticides, and other aids that would increase agricultural productivity.

INTERNATIONAL COOPERATION IN
SCIENCE AND TECHNOLOGY

International cooperation may take several forms, including regional, bilateral, or multilateral agreements between advanced and developing countries or between different developing countries. A prime consideration in the adoption of any scheme of cooperation is that the developing country or countries should be free from external pressures from the countries with which they are cooperating.

Regional Institutes

Regional institutes appear to offer great advantages in developing countries. The problems of countries in the same ecological zone are often identical or similar. Pooling resources for the investigation of problems in one regional center, serving a number of countries, is an obvious way of circumventing the inadequate manpower and material resources of single countries. Certain precautions, however, need to be taken if these centers are to fulfill the objectives they seek. Thus, they must not be such as to draw away scientists who are required for work in national institutes. To avoid this, service in regional institutes must be on a temporary basis, with arrangements for rotation of staff with national institutes. The work in a regional institute must clearly be different from that being carried out in national institutes.

Centers of Excellence

An instrument for the development of high scientific research standards is the "center of excellence." A particular form of this involves the partial staffing of a well-endowed and adequately equipped center with an international cadre of post doctoral fellows from more-developed countries who would spend a year or two in the developing country, working alongside qualified nationals. High academic standards would be secured by the participation, on a part time basis, of eminent scientists from developed countries. It is envisaged that ultimately the center would come entirely under the control of qualified and experienced nationals. Such a center of excellence in steroid chemistry has been of outstanding scientific and economic value in Mexico.

Contacts Between Scientists

Other useful forms of regional cooperation include the exchange of experts in various fields, frequent and regular meetings between them, the systematic exchange of information between appropriate agencies, meetings of science administrators from universities and research institutes, and the provision of facilities to enable scientists from one country in the region to pursue their interests in another, as well as to participate in international conferences and congresses.

International Cooperation in Training and Research

International cooperation, particularly between developed and developing countries, can help significantly to provide solutions for some of the most acute problems facing the poorer countries—namely, shortage of personnel for manning training and research institutions and lack of funds for purchasing equipment. Significant contributions can and have been made by schemes of multilateral assistance through the United Nations and other agencies.

A valuable form of assistance to training institutions is that which establishes a cooperative link between an institution, usually a university, in a developed country and a corresponding institution in a developing country. This link could embrace the provision and/or exchange of staff and collaboration in research programs.

International cooperation, particularly through multilateral schemes under the aegis of UNESCO, has an important part to play in the modernization of science teaching schools. Such cooperation could take the form of the development of mechanisms for the prompt and regular transmission of the products of curriculum-development studies conducted in one country to other countries, the provision of facilities for personnel from one country to observe or participate in curriculum-development efforts in other countries, and the sponsoring of regional projects of curriculum and syllabus reform, such as the UNESCO projects on the teaching of biology, chemistry, and physics conducted in Africa, Asia, and Latin America, respectively.

Other forms of international assistance could include the provision of personnel, funds, and equipment for important research and other technical projects in all fields. There is a great need for the recipient countries to exercise extreme caution to ensure that projects receiving such assistance, often requiring matching effort by the recipient, deserve priority attention at the time and are not merely projects of interest to the "donor" countries alone.

NATURAL RESOURCES

Natural resources, including man himself and all the components of his environment that can be utilized to improve his welfare and well-being, form the basis for all development. It has been accepted, therefore, that their exploration and exploitation provide the foundation upon which all other developmental activities must rest.

Exploitation requires, in the first instance, the survey of resources to ascertain their location, quantity, and quality. Planning on the basis of surveys requires an appreciation of long- and short-term needs. Thus, a particular resource may have to be exploited in advance of knowledge of the full extent of its occurrence throughout the country—a mineral deposit or a water source, for example, that may be urgently required to meet a pressing need. Otherwise, the exploitation of natural resources must be based, as far as possible, on integrated plans for development, which in turn call for a more comprehensive view.

Due regard must also be given to the important concept of conservation—namely, utilization of the resources in such a manner as not to squander them through the neglect of the long-term interests of the country. Thus, a nonrenewable resource, such as a mineral deposit, must be exploited at a controlled rate, taking into account the dangers of overproduction on the value of the world markets and of the prospects of increasing value in the long term. For a renewable underground water source, the rate of utilization should take into account the rate of recharge. The objective of conservation is exploitation under conditions ensuring a maximum sustained yield.

The Land Surface: Mapping

An essential requirement for compiling an over-all picture of natural resources in a country is the existence of adequate maps. The compilation of maps of different scales would involve the use of aerial photography and photogrammetry, as well as survey on the ground. A survey department manned by adequately trained surveyors, photogrammetrists, and technicians must be built up.

Mineral Resources

Most countries have large unexploited and uncharted mineral resources, the survey and evaluation of which must be undertaken by a combination of geological mapping and exploration and detailed laboratory studies. Systematic geological mapping and exploration are slow and time-consuming undertakings, and great benefit may be derived by the use of modern methods of geophysical and geochemical exploration. There is need for mineral-processing laboratories to conduct research on the value of ores in order to meet the demand for higher-grade and better-prepared products.

To produce persons capable of making immediate contributions to the solution of practical problems, training programs should be so designed as to utilize experience gained outside the university—that is, in industry.

Water Resources

Measures, including the setting up of meteorological and hydro-
logic services, should be instituted for the survey and evaluation of
water resources. Prospecting should be undertaken for underground
water, using aerial photography and geophysical methods, to be followed by drilling to prove and evaluate the extent of reserves. Methods
for determining the rates and direction of flow of underground water
and of establishing connections between different water sources need
study by geophysical methods and the use of radioactive and stable
tracers. Methods for preventing evaporation and seepage from reser-
voirs and canals, as well as for the more economical use of water,
must be devised. In particular, the breeding of plant varieties with
minimal water requirements and also of salt-resistant varieties
capable of growth in brackish water deserve attention.

Artificial methods of obtaining water, such as by inducing rainfall by seeding and the desalination of salt water, may be crucial in
arid regions. Desalination by distillation is now a practical reality,
although the cost of the water may still be prohibitive. The combination of a desalination plant with a heat-generating plant, such as a
thermal- or nuclear-power station, may reduce this cost considerably.

Energy

Prospecting must be undertaken in all countries for conventional
energy sources—fossil fuels, including coal, lignite, petroleum, and
gas—and for hydroelectric potential. Where isolated rural communities are involved, nonconventional sources, such as "biogas" (mixture
of combustible gases produced by rotting vegetable wastes), solar
energy, or geothermal energy, may be exploited. Particularly for
isolated countries in arid regions without abundant reserves of fossil
fuels or hydroelectric potential, solar energy may be the preferred
source. Considerable progress has been made in its utilization for
many domestic purposes, such as cooking, water heating, heating of
homes, refrigeration, and for drying agricultural produce. More
research is needed into its use for the direct generation of electricity
an as economic proposition. Geothermal energy, the energy in hot
gases and steam that issues from the ground in certain localities in
the world, is a source that has been successfully used in such countries as New Zealand and Italy.

Nuclear energy is believed by many to be an important energy
source for the future, especially in countries that have no fossil fuels
or hydroelectric potential. For large outputs of power (500-1,000
MW), the cost of electricity generated by nuclear plants is now

competitive with that generated by thermal-power plants. The disadvantages of nuclear power, as far as developing countries are concerned, are the high capital costs and the large outputs of economical generating plants. Such large outputs must be absorbed by the creation of large industrial systems, which require much larger investments than needed for the nuclear plant itself. Other disadvantages are the high level of technical expertise required to operate nuclear plants, and problems relating to the supply of fuel. It is believed that the latter may be solved by the development of fast breeder reactors, which produce more fuel than they consume. In spite of these difficulties, certain developing countries, such as India, Thailand, the U.A.R., South Korea, and Taiwan, have either built or ordered nuclear generators, and others may follow their example. It is argued in certain quarters that it would be more rational, eventually, to generate electric power by nuclear plants and reserve oil and natural gas for the petrochemical industries.

Integrated River-Basin Development

The development of river basins in an integrated plan is believed to offer great advantages. It is a concept that has proved its value in many river valleys of the world. A project might include the integrated development of hydroelectric power, irrigation, soil conservation, river transport, flood control, recreational facilities, and fisheries. The magnitude of the investment required may be an obstacle in many developing countries, but efforts should be made, whenever possible, to solicit international aid.

A sensible approach to the project requires the drawing up, at the outset, of overall plans, which must be flexible to allow for changes dictated by developments as implementation proceeds. Since such schemes usually involve severe dislocations in the life of the people in the area, implementation should be preceded and continuously accompanied by intensive and sound educational programs to help them adjust to and make the best use of the facilities—for example, improved water supplies, electricity, and farming potential—the scheme provides.

The Soil

The soil is the basis of all arable agriculture. Its successful utilization must be based on a knowledge of the different types of soils and their distribution. Studies of their physical, chemical, and biological properties must also be undertaken so that they can be classified according to capability. Assessment of capability should take into account whether cultivation is to be by hand, by mechanization, by irrigation, or under some other conditions of water availability.

Equally important are long-term studies on the effects of fertilizer application under different moisture and other conditions and its suitability for particular crops and cultivation practices. Methods for preventing erosion can be enhanced by knowledge of soil-conservation practices in both developed and developing countries.

Plant Resources: Agriculture

The bulk of the population in most developing countries is engaged in agriculture. Productivity is usually low because of the primitive methods used. The importance of agriculture as a means of producing food and raw materials for local industries and for export requires that it receive special attention. In most developing countries, the crying need is for the modernization of agricultural methods. Among the measures that will bring about increases in productivity are application of fertilizers; provision of water, in many cases by irrigation; cropping systems that bring about speedy regeneration of the soil; the selection and breeding of better and improved varieties; and sensible mechanization, using machines and implements suitable for the ecological and sociological conditions that obtain.

There is also need to apply measures for protection of crops from pests and diseases. These would be based on a firm understanding of the ecological relationships between the different organisms present and on sound research into plant pathology and entomology.

Other Natural Resources

Other important natural resources that need to be studied and conservatively exploited are livestock, forests, fish, and wildlife. The conclusions reached and recommendations made about the development and exploitation of these resources are fully discussed by L. K. H. Goma in Chapter 5.

INDUSTRIALIZATION

The importance of industrialization as an essential stage in the utilization of natural resources has been emphasized. The manufacture of mineral and agricultural raw materials into finished products is a means of achieving a certain measure of independence from the industrial systems of the developed countries, as well as a means of procuring capital for other forms of development. Industrialization can also provide certain essential basic requirements for the modernization of agriculture.

Transfer of Technology

Industrialization is one main area in which much can be achieved by the direct transfer of technology, with or without adaptation as appropriate, from developed countries. Of primary importance is the machinery for the transfer of know-how, such as a "technology transfer center," an integrated government-sponsored organization that will make available to potential users information as to where a particular technology may be obtained and give assistance in gaining access to that technology and that will advise industrialists as to which technology will best meet their objectives. Such a center may also indicate ways in which the technology may be adapted to local conditions. It should be staffed with a team of competent experienced technologists who possess the dynamism and contacts to direct inquiries to appropriate sources of information and help.

Appropriate Industries and Manufactures

A major consideration in plans for industrialization must be the development of industries that are appropriate to the particular circumstances of the country. One aid in this connection is the establishment of an industrial research institute to determine the use of local materials.

There is need also for investigations into the design and manufacture of machinery and equipment specifically adapted to the conditions in the developing country. This will remove difficulties arising from the importation of unsuitable equipment designed for conditions obtaining in countries with different physical and sociological conditions.

Important areas in which industries could be established are food processing and preservation, processing of animal and vegetable products not used for food (for example, plywood, paper, skins, and hides), metals, fertilizers and heavy chemicals, including petrochemicals, and building materials from local raw materials.

Protein Foods from Industrial Processes

Special mention needs to be made of the manufacture of protein-rich foods from industrial processes. Thus, oil-seed-crushing—for example, of ground nuts—produces press cake for feeding animals and protein concentrates particularly suitable for infants. Another source of proteinaceous food has recently been discovered in microbial metabolites that grow on petroleum as a source of carbon.

Animal-feeding experiments have shown that the product has a high value as a protein food. A great deal of work has been done on the extraction of protein from leaves. Highly nutritious foods have been obtained, but more attention is required to convert them into products acceptable to human beings.

Industrial Standards

The maintenance of high standards of manufacture, essential for products for home and export markets, requires the setting up of appropriate machinery, such as an industrial-standards board. The major task of such a board will be to establish specifications and standards for the control of raw materials and of manufactured products. Most of the basic information exists in developed countries and could be adapted to suit conditions. A certain amount of experimental work will have to be undertaken, but this could be combined with the testing and verification of standards as a means of checking manufactured goods against declared standards and specifications.

HEALTH

Most of the developing countries have similar health problems: a high incidence of communicable diseases; deficiency diseases trace-able to malnutrition, especially protein malnutrition; high maternal and infant mortality; deficient environmental sanitation (inadequate water supplies, refuse and sewage disposal, and housing).

Planning for tackling these problems requires information about the population, including distribution between different age groups, births and deaths, and the incidence of various diseases. A basic activity should be research into methods of carrying out statistical investigations that provide short cuts to the assembly of full and accurate statistics.

In addition, intensive efforts employing known methods must be made—particularly immunization, control of insect vectors, and treatment with drugs—and research carried out on more effective measures, including new vaccines, new drugs, and a fuller under-standing of the behavior of the various vectors.

Planning of Health Services

Since the bulk of the populations in most developing countries live in rural areas, realistic health-service planning will provide not only for urban centers but also for the villages. In this, prevention of disease by the provision of clean water supplies and sanitation must receive at least as much attention as provision for the treatment of illness.

Training of Health Personnel

Health personnel, doctors, nurses, sanitarians, and others must be trained with the local situations in mind and, hence, in institutions in the developing countries themselves. The different patterns of disease from those encountered in developed countries must be borne in mind. Thus, there must be proper emphasis on preventive medicine, embracing public health and hygiene and the control of communicable diseases. The doctor must be trained to understand the health needs of his community and be oriented to promote health in its wider and positive sense of physical, mental, and social well-being, rather than the mere absence of disease.

SPECIAL RESPONSIBILITIES OF SCIENTISTS

Ethical Problems

The Pugwash conferences have been concerned with the special responsibilities of the sciences, primarily those that relate to ethical problems. It has been argued that scientists have a special obligation to humanity over and above those of nonscientists, by virtue of the potential for both good and evil that is inherent in their activities. Scientists should accept the social consequences of their actions. This obliges them to seek closer communication with politicians in order to make them aware of the long-range implications of particular scientific tools.

Many of the ethical problems of science have answers that must involve not only the physical and biological sciences, but also the social sciences and the humanities. Thus, practitioners of the two areas must work toward unifying their social aims.

Scientists As Advisers to Governments

Scientific advice to governments must be critical and independent, rather than merely informative, and governments should be encouraged to take action upon the advice, not of single individuals, but of national scientific bodies. Scientists should also seek to educate governments

to give due weight to the opinions of local scientists, rather than
accept outside advice or criticism in preference.

Scientists and Public Opinion

Scientists have an obligation to project a true picture of science
as a process of discovery mainly by trial and error, rather than an
inexorable process with mystical qualities. They are further obliged
to inform not only their colleagues but also the general public of the
results of their work. They should not hesitate to use the communications media to convey scientific ideas and principles in simple terms.
The entire population has to move with the advancing frontiers of
science and must be given the opportunity to do so.

The Scientists' Role in Education

It is yet another obligation of scientists to inform themselves of
the evolving attitudes toward science education and the new techniques
that are being developed throughout the world. They should also,
whenever possible, make sure that curricula, syllabuses, and teaching
materials, including textbooks, are not only up to date but also display
the fascination of discovery and stimulate curiosity.

Science textbooks can be a means of eliminating barriers between
nations and increasing mutual understanding. By incorporating an
outline of the history and philosophy of science, textbooks and courses
can impart to the student a feeling of the world to which he belongs and
help toward the creation of a sense of world citizenship.

5

SCIENCE
AND TECHNOLOGY
IN AFRICAN
ECONOMIC
DEVELOPMENT
L. K. H. Goma

It is generally agreed that accelerated economic development in Africa is particularly inhibited by the serious lag in scientific and technological advances in the African context. It is also clear that African countries vary in their natural-resource endowments, the structure of their economies, their capabilities, and thus their future objectives. In these circumstances, the extent to which science and technology can contribute to economic development will differ from one country to another.

There are two aspects to the utilization of science and technology in the economic development of any developing area. The first constitutes the application and adaptation of existing knowledge, obtainable from the developed countries of the world; the second involves the acquisition of new knowledge within the developing area itself and especially suited to the unique conditions of the area. This chapter makes no distinction between the two, its purpose being to attempt to establish the role of science and technology (whether borrowed or indigenous or both) in African economic development. The discussion that follows will concentrate on this role in the context of agricultural production, improvement of health, exploitation of natural resources, industrialization, and transportation and communications.

AGRICULTURAL PRODUCTION

Throughout most of Africa the overwhelming majority of people are directly engaged in agriculture and will continue to be so in the decades to come. In general, they are extremely poor. For them, economic progress must necessarily depend on a new agricultural technology. [1]

The African natural environment imposes on agriculture certain inherent difficulties. African soils are generally poor; in many parts, the rainfall is both deficient and unreliable; vast areas of land are arid or semiarid. Then, too, there are the problems of heat stress for farm animals, high fiber content in the feed for cattle, formidable animal diseases, and devastating crop pests. These factors hamper agricultural progress severely in that they set limits to the type of crop that can be grown, planting dates, and the type of livestock to be raised, as well as the grazing available for them. It has been shown, however, that science and technology can and already do play a crucial role in the solution of these problems and that the African environment can produce thoroughly satisfactory yields if it is managed with knowledge and understanding.

The Soil

As no satisfactory and definite substitute appears to have been found for bush fallow as a means of maintaining soil fertility, more extensive fertility research is indicated.[2] In addition to soil chemistry, soil physics and soil biology need to be more fully explored. An understanding of the conditions of the soil is crucial if crop yields are to be increased and the soil and its beneficial biotic communities properly conserved.[3]

The Crops

In the field of crop production, there is need to develop new individual breeds of crops or to improve existing ones so that they can be better adapted to given physical, chemical, and biological conditions of the environment. Already in East Africa, for instance, a great deal of work has been carried out on the development of drought-tolerant grain crops for use in arid areas.[4] This work could be increased in scope and value, however, by basic physiological and biochemical factors that enable these varieties to succeed. Similar advances have been made in the improvement of a number of major cash crops in various African countries, such as maize, coffee, tea, cocoa, wheat, oil palm, tobacco, and cotton, some of which have been a major factor in economic development.

It is clear, however, that until comparatively recently most of the crops to which scientific and technological attention was devoted previously were those developed primarily for the export trade. There remains work to be done on the yield and quality of more of the basic food crops for home consumption and/or for the local food-processing industries.

The Livestock

In a number of African countries, the potential for animal production, both for export and for home consumption or local industries, is enormous; yet many of them have to import meat, milk, and butter. It is also a fact that the indigenous tropical breeds of cattle, for example, generally have a low productivity, while the highly productive temperate breeds undergo progressive deterioration when introduced into the tropics. [5] There is obviously an urgent need to conduct substantial investigations into the nutritional, physiological, pathological, and environmental factors that may be limiting the breeding efficiencies of farm animals. [6] As indigenous breeds generally make better use of local feedstuffs, show greater resistance to extremes of weather and to disease, and have more stable calving rates, the efficiency of their husbandry might be increased through selective breeding. [7] On the other hand, better results might be achieved through cross-breeding between the indigenous and the imported high breeds. Thus, animal genetics and breeding could play an important role in improving livestock production in Africa.

There is also need to expand and intensify pasture research in order to raise the value, as well as the carrying capacity, of pasture land. With regard to livestock diseases, there have been some noteworthy achievements in their control. Among those that still exist, however, are East Coast fever, hoof-and-mouth disease, rinderpest, contagious bovine pleuropneumonia, and trypanosomiasis (nagana). This last disease, transmitted by the tsetse fly, is perhaps the greatest single impediment to the development of the stock-raising industry in Africa today: large areas of otherwise suitable grazing land are at present denied to cattle. [8]

IMPROVEMENT OF HEALTH

People whose energies are sapped by ill-health are unlikely to advance themselves economically. Among the most serious impediments to African economic development have been the many tropical diseases found on the continent, such as malaria, bilharzia, and sleeping sickness. To these scourges should be added protein-calorie malnutrition.

Malaria

Of all the major tropical endemic diseases, malaria is certainly that with the most serious repercussions on the death rate and on economics. In Africa, malaria is a great debilitating disease of the masses, and its influence on the distribution of human populations and their movements, agriculture, industry, education, and general social well-being has been far-reaching. [9] The effective control or eradication of the disease is dependent not so much on curative measures as on the control or eradication of the mosquito vector. This objective, however, can be achieved only through biological research and application. Unfortunately, even in the developed countries, success in this area has been minimal.

Bilharzia

In Africa, bilharzia is as widespread and debilitating a disease as malaria. The intermediate snail hosts inhabit fresh water and so there is a complication here—water-resource conservation, hydro-electric development schemes, and large-scale extension of irrigation increase the potential of this disease.

At the present time, only control of the intermediate snail hosts will eradicate the disease. Whether this is accomplished by molluscicides or by biological measures, however, there must first be sound knowledge of the ecology, seasonal distribution, and other population dynamics of the snails. Such knowledge is grossly inadequate at the present time, even with recent advances in chemotherapy.

Sleeping Sickness

Reference has already been made to the harmful effects of the tsetse fly, the vector of sleeping sickness, or human trypanosomiasis, on the stock-raising industry. This insect has for countless years effectively prevented man from occupying extensive areas of the continent. Although spectacular successes have been achieved in some localized campaigns against it, there is alarming evidence that it is advancing along several fronts and occupying new territory. [10]

There exists a considerable body of knowledge on trypanosomiasis and the vectors of the disease. Progress in chemotherapy and chemoprophylaxis has made it possible to reduce the severity of, and even prevent, epidemics. But until transmission can be broken or brought under effective control, the disease will remain a threat to health and prevent large tracts of country from being utilized for agricultural purposes. [11]

Malnutrition

One of the most widespread and serious childhood diseases in Africa and in other developing areas of the world, malnutrition is nevertheless easily preventable. Success in combating the disease demands the combined efforts of specialists belonging to a wide range of disciplines: medical officers, agriculturists, biochemists, food technologists, sociologists, administrators, and industrialists. There is an obvious need for research on the production of more protein-rich foods at acceptable costs, as well as on the identification and elimination of toxins produced by contaminating fungi. [12]

EXPLOITATION OF NATURAL RESOURCES

The importance of natural resources for economic development is universally recognized. In the case of Africa, this matter was the subject of considerable discussion at the United Nations Economic, Scientific and Cultural Organization/Economic Commission for Africa (UNESCO-ECA) International Conference on the Organization of Research and Training in Africa in Relation to the Study, Conservation, and Utilization of Natural Resources, Lagos, 1964. It is clear, however, that the natural resources of Africa, both renewable and nonrenewable, are not being fully exploited for economic development. There is still a great deal to know about them: their location; physical, chemical, or biological characteristics; economic potential; and so on. Scientists and technologists involved in this effort may consider the problem in terms of: mineral resources, water and energy resources, and biological resources.

Mineral Resources

Africa has reasonably abundant and varied mineral resources, some of which rank as the major deposits of their type in the world. [13] These include the gold deposits of Ghana and South Africa, the copper deposits of Zambia and Congo (Kinshasa), the iron deposits of Liberia, the diamond deposits of Sierra Leone, and the phosphate deposits of Morocco. These deposits, however, do not last forever, and eventually production from them must be supplemented from other, perhaps less well-known, deposits. The exploitation of these resources has been and will probably continue to be the only rapid way open to some African countries to bypass the laborious process of economic growth through agricultural development. [14]

An understanding of the basic geology and structure of a country is of vital importance not only to the search for new minerals, but also to the provision of essential information required in a variety of other undertakings. By now, the major features of the geology of Africa are known, but, aside from a few areas like the Witwatersrand in South Africa and the Congo (Kinshasa)-Zambia copper belt, most of the continent has not been investigated in great detail.[15] In recent years, prospecting methods have been improved as a result of new techniques in geophysics and geochemistry. These are particularly important in Africa, where direct geological research is difficult and expensive, owing to the forest cover or the sand or laterite overburden in many areas. The search for minerals is one thing; however, their exploitation is another. Just as modern technology has advanced the former, so must it be effectively applied to the latter.

Water and Energy Resources

The development of water resources is crucial, not only for higher standards of sanitation and health, but also for agricultural and industrial growth.[16] For there to be progress in this area, however, there is need to have reliable hydrological maps (at present, few countries in Africa have these, and most have none at all),[17] to undertake research in hydraulics and soil mechanics, and to investigate the quality and availability of ground water, as well as more effective means of preventing water losses through evaporation and seepage. In these investigations, and wherever possible, full use should be made of such modern techniques as isotopes and computers, as well as of data from aerial photographs. Modern well-recording procedures and improved drilling equipment would permit better identification, assessment, and development of underground water resources.

Africa has vast areas with arid or semiarid conditions that permit only one agricultural crop a year, if at all. In these areas, the development of surface and underground water for irrigation may not only increase the yield but also make it possible to grow two or even three crops a year. Moreover, it is conceivable that totally new crops could be introduced.

There is an increasing demand in Africa for electric energy, for both domestic and industrial purposes. The basic and most economic source of this energy is to be found in the as yet undeveloped hydroelectric potential of the continent's major rivers.[18] Other sources of energy that may be utilized with equal success in particular areas are the fossil fuels—coal, oil, and natural gas. For the Sahara, Nigeria, and Gabon, for example, oil and possibly natural gas may become the main sources of energy.

Biological Resources

The biological natural resources of Africa that can be exploited economically consist fundamentally of plants and animals. Development of these resources, however, has of necessity nearly always been undertaken with scant knowledge. [19] In the long run, it is essential that the biological potential either of the area itself or of neighboring areas remains unimpaired by the processes of development; to date, however, there has been little chance of establishing with certainty what effect such processes will have on the landscape. For present purposes, the exploitable biological natural resources are considered under the main headings of forestry, fisheries, and wildlife (wild-game animals).

The role of forestry in the development of Africa, as elsewhere, is twofold and includes, on the one hand, the protection of water catchments, the provision of windbreaks, and the conservation of existing water supplies and, on the other, the exploitation of trees, both exotic and indigenous, for the production of timber and timber products. [20] Although there have been considerable achievements in this field, much work remains to be undertaken: indigenous and plantation silviculture, forest genetics and ecology, tree physiology and taxonomy, studies of wood diseases and wood quality, and general forest-products research.

The fishes of Africa are in many parts of the continent the most valuable natural resource, in terms of both food and hard cash. A proper utilization of this resource could, therefore, make an immense difference to the solution of the protein-calorie malnutrition problem discussed above. The fishes also play an important part in the tourist industry and in the recreational requirements of the countries.

Fundamental and applied biological research on the fishes of Africa must contribute to the development of the fishing industry. The fisherman would like to know if he is fishing in the most profitable locality, if he is using the most efficient type of net to catch the fish, if the stock of fish is increasing or decreasing, and if the excessive fishing at point A is likely to destroy the stock fished at point B. These are questions about the distribution, behavior, population dynamics, and migration of fish that only biological investigations can answer.

The utilization of wildlife as an integral part of Africa's economy is becoming increasingly important, as its tourist industry shows. The remarkable richness and abundance of tropical Africa's mammal fauna, however, also represents a considerable potential food resource. It has been claimed that on comparable land, other things being equal, the harvest of meat from wild animals should be several times greater than that from domestic livestock under the conditions

found in most of Africa. [21] One of the immediate needs in many parts
of the continent today is a regular supply of cheap meat, and game-
cropping holds much promise in this direction.

Correct wildlife-management programs, however, can be formulated only when the relevant factors—such as the growth characteristics,
breeding and mortality rates, optimum sex and age ratios, and the
food requirements of each type of animal—have been determined and
the structure, state, and requirements of the vegetation (in the
environment) understood. [22]

INDUSTRIALIZATION

The desire of most African governments is to try to industrialize
their nations as rapidly as possible. They realize that progress in
agriculture (which affects the lives of the overwhelming majority of
the people in their respective countries, as indicated above) is bound
to be slow, because there is still too much to be known as to the best
means of improving agricultural production and increasing the productivity of subsistence farmers. On the other hand, a great deal of the
necessary skill and technology in industry is easily transferable from
the advanced countries to Africa. For most African countries, however, the range of possibilities for industrialization in the immediate
future is not very great. These comments and those that follow relate
to manufacturing industries, rather than to the production of raw
materials for processing and manufacture abroad. Because of the
heterogeneous nature of the conditions in Africa, it is clear that the
industrial mix in most, if not all, of the countries must span a range
from village and handicraft industries using no power to large industrial undertakings employing modern technology, substantial power,
and concentration of high-level manpower. It is the latter that are
discussed here.

Food-Manufacturing Industries

There is a great need in many parts of Africa to set up these
industries, using the available local agricultural, as well as natural,
products. Apart from offering employment to the vast numbers of
people now unemployed, this should serve to cut down the importation
of similar foods from abroad and also help to reduce the considerable
wastage of food products owing to inadequate facilities for preservation
at present. [23] It is essential, however, that there be proper investigations of such problems as the general nutritional needs of the people;
the extent to which traditional methods of storage and processing can
be improved through the use of such modern methods as canning,

refrigeration, and dehydration; the retention of nutritive value in stored and processed food; and the production of new high-protein foods.

Chemical and Allied Industries

The growth of new chemical industries depends primarily on the existence of a basic industry to produce the chemicals for large-scale use. The provision of such a chemical as sulphuric acid could, for instance, lead to the manufacture of phosphate fertilizer and aluminum sulphate, which is used in large quantities for the purification of water and deodorization of sewage systems. Many African countries produce no sulphuric acid at present, but deposits of sulphide minerals from which it could be derived are known to exist.

The immense deposits of phosphate in parts of Africa are required for agricultural fertilizing. It is not enough, however, to dig up the calcium phosphate and then spread it on the fields: it has to be converted into the product known as superphosphate, in which form it is available for the growth of plants. [24] To do this, large quantities of sulphuric acid are required. The development of the phosphate-fertilizer industry is thus linked up with the manufacture and supply of sulphuric acid. Where oil refineries are available, these could contribute to the production of other fertilizers, although they may not provide the basis of a complete fertilizer industry.

Many parts of Africa have considerable deposits of clay suitable for the manufacture of bricks, tiles, tube ware, and pottery and of other minerals for white ware and porcelain. In most of these countries, however, ceramics research is grossly inadequate to permit the full use of these resources.

Agricultural and Industrial Waste Conversion

There is a wide field of presently unutilized waste from agricultural activities, forests, fisheries, and various industries. Efforts to find commercially economic uses for this waste might include the manufacture of paper from bagasse, grasses, and bamboo.

Miscellaneous Industries

Several other industries that have been and could be established by using modern technologies developed elsewhere and suitably adapted to the African situation are: the manufacture of textiles, leather and leather products, insecticides and pesticides, pharmaceuticals, building materials and construction, and metal products and equipment. Many of the countries can and do produce the basic raw materials in most cases. Again, apart from offering employment to those in need, these endeavors could cut down imports and reduce current foreign-exchange and reserve problems.

TRANSPORTATION AND COMMUNICATIONS

An effective transportation and communications system is a necessary condition for rapid economic development in any country. It serves to link all the other sectors of the economy together and has a profound influence on the achievements in almost every sphere of national life. The development efforts of most African countries severely suffer from the lack of adequate transportation and communication facilities. This unsatisfactory situation is true of all the main modes of transportation and communications: roads, railways, water transport, and air transport.

Roads and Road Transport

For most African countries, roads and road transport provide an ideal means of connecting the widely scattered rural communities, opening up new areas to development, widening the domestic market, and performing the diverse types of transport functions related to the process of industrialization and economic growth. It is first necessary, however, to evolve patterns of road-building that are suited to the local climatic conditions and that will make the best use of local materials. A major problem in Africa and in other developing areas is that of gathering information about the occurrence and properties of the road-making materials.[25] Here, the engineer can work with the geologist and the pedologist in delineating the soil variations that are significant and with the physicist and the chemist in defining the properties of the different types of soils. There are numerous other factors relating not only to road-building materials and ground conditions of the terrain, but also to the structural design of roads, the elucidation of which calls for cooperation between different types of scientific and technological investigators.

Railways

Railways have played an increasingly vital role in the development of a number of countries in Africa. Where heavy volumes of bulk commodities, particularly minerals, are to be moved over long distances and no water transportation is available, the railroad almost invariably will be the most economical choice. For some countries, what is required is concentration on the modernization of their equipment, adoption of modern techniques, and improvement of their operating efficiency. For others, there is every justification for large-scale building of new railway lines, which will demand the combined efforts of the engineer, the geologist, the pedologist, the physicist, and the geographer.

Water Transport

Waterways, like railways, can be a highly economical and effective means in the movement of mineral and agricultural products involving bulk transportation. At present, there would seem to be a need for considerable hydrographic surveys and other investigations of inland waterways, so that realistic development programs can be undertaken in this direction.

Air Transport

The long distances and the slowness of what ground transport exists in Africa emphasize the need for civil aviation as an effective means of handling high-speed traffic. Apart from its expensiveness, however, the operation of this form of transportation is a highly technical matter, requiring high-level skills in civil engineering, aeronautical engineering, and meteorology. In the construction of air fields, the problems of structural design, materials, ground conditions, and so on, are fairly similar to those discussed above in connection with roads, and their solution demands the attention of scientists and technologists in the same general fields.

CONCLUSIONS

In considering the role of science and technology in African economic development, it is important to distinguish between what is theoretically possible and what is practically possible. In this regard, attention should be drawn to certain key factors that may limit the proper application of these disciplines.

A most critical limitation on the capacity of a country to absorb and apply new techniques is its supply of trained manpower. It is clear that the institutions and resources now available in the various African countries are too limited to produce the scientific and technological manpower on the scale required for more-rapid economic

development. The lack of proper manpower-planning in most of these
countries and the laissez-faire approach to the selection and training
of students in the universities and colleges aggravate the situation.
In addition, what manpower is available is ineffectively utilized. Reliance on costly expatriate skills can be regarded only as a stopgap
measure. The production of the needed skills, in a balanced manner,
is a critical task that must be assigned to and accepted by the African
universities and colleges. The quota system is an obvious means of
achieving this objective. Greater use should also be made of the
expertise concentrated in the universities and colleges.

A second major limiting factor in the application of science and
technology is lack of funds. Most African countries are poor and
must make hard choices. They must find the techniques that impose
the least sacrifices or be forced to deny themselves the modernization
that science and technology can make possible. The conditions imposed
on borrowing money from abroad may be totally unacceptable, in which
case regional cooperation among African countries would be the only
satisfactory answer.

Then, there are the social and psychological barriers to technological change. As was pointed out at the Nineteenth Pugwash Conference in Nice, 1968, ignorance of what is attainable through science
and technology, coupled with insufficient decolonization of the mind
and the consequent uncritical adulation of foreign experts and know-
how, obscure attitudes on the part of even some local scientists, and
the fact that industry is often in the hands of nonnationals or based on
foreign collaboration may lead not only to a lack of or insufficient
demand for research in the various sectors of the national economy
and militate against the effective use of the limited human resources,
but also to the application of inappropriate technologies in the developing world, the African countries included. [26]

The conclusion that progress in science and technology, in the
African context, can contribute significantly, even decisively, to
economic development cannot be challenged. The many and extremely
serious obstacles to realization of this goal must not be minimized,
however.

NOTES

1. A. H. Bunting, "The Role of the Universities in Rural
Development," Report of the Malta Conference of Overseas Vice-
Chancellors and Principals, 1969 (unpublished).

2. P. F. M. McLoughlin, "Some Technical Research Problems for Agricultural Development in Tropical Africa," Development Digest, V, 1967, pp. 123-32.

3. W. B. Banage, "Biological Aspects of Soil Research," Research Priorities for East Africa: Contemporary African Monograph No. 5 (Nairobi: East African Institute of Social and Cultural Affairs, 1966), pp. 47-53.

4. O. Starnes, "Priorities in Agricultural Research," Research Priorities, op. cit., pp. 36-46.

5. E. B. Galukande, "The Genetics of Milk Production in East Africa," Proceedings of the East African Academy, I, 1964, pp. 133-36.

6. P. C. Nderito, "Problems of Livestock Development," Research Priorities, op. cit., pp. 66-72.

7. D. P. S. Wasawo, "The Importance of Research in the Biological Sciences to the Development of East Africa" (Nairobi: East African Academy, 1966), pp. 77-92.

8. United Nations Economic and Social Council, Third Report of the Advisory Committee on the Application of Science and Technology to Development, Supplement No. 12, 1966.

9. L. K. H. Goma, "The Mosquito," in Tropical Monographs (London: Hutchinson, 1966); and M. H. Holstein, Biology of the Anopheles Gambiae, W.H.O. Monograph No. 9 (Geneva, 1954).

10. World Health Organization, "Trypanosomiasis Control in Africa," W.H.O. Chronicle, XVII, 1963, pp. 43-49.

11. R. J. Onyango, "Medical Research Priorities for Tropical Diseases," Research Priorities, op. cit., pp. 21-24.

12. F. J. Bennett and D. Bradley, "Public Health Research in Africa," Research Priorities, op. cit., pp. 25-30.

13. L. R. Page, "Earth Sciences in African Development," Proceedings of the East African Academy, II, 1964, pp. 46-49.

14. A. M. Karmack, The Economics of African Development (New York: Praeger, 1967).

15. Ibid.

16. Proceedings of 15th Pugwash Conference on Science and World Affairs, 1966.

17. L. Berry, "Geographical Research in East Africa," in Research and Development in East Africa (Nairobi: East African Academy, 1966), pp. 92-97.

18. Karmack, African Development; and S. R. Smith, "Programme for Hydro-electric Development in West Africa to 1980," W. M. Warren and N. Rubin, eds., Dams in Africa (London: Cass, 1968), pp. 158-88.

19. E. W. Russell, "Respective Role of Research and Technical Services in the Inventorying of Natural Resources, Their Evaluation, Improvement and Present Exploitation, and in Devising New Ways of Utilizing Them," (UNESCO/CORPSA/DISC. 1), UNESCO-ECA Conference, Lagos, 1964.

20. L. K. H. Goma, "The Biologist in Africa," Distinguished Guest Lecture No. 2 (unpublished) (Nairobi: East African Academy, 1967).

21. F. L. Lambrecht, "Some Principles of Tsetse Control," East African Wildlife Journal, IV, 1966.

22. W. R. Bambridge, "The Reaping of the Game Harvest in Zambia," Zambia, January, 1967, pp. 39-46.

23. J. Yanney-Ewusie, "The Organization, Technical and Scientific Internal Functioning and Programmes of Bodies Carrying Out Research in the Field of Mineral Resources and of Basic Industries," (UNESCO/CORPSA/DISC. 6 A), UNESCO-ECA Conference, Lagos, 1965, pp. 89-99.

24. M. Crawford, "Chemical Research and the Development of Natural Product Resources in East Africa," R. J. Olembo, ed., Human Adaptation in Tropical Africa (East African Academy, 1968), pp. 71-80.

25. R. Jones, "The Importance of Research in Civil Engineering to the Development of East Africa," in Research and Development in East Africa (Nairobi: East African Academy, 1966), pp. 66-67.

26. R. S. Eckaus, "Technological Change in the Less Developed Areas," in Development of the Emerging Countries (Washington, D.C.: Brookings, 1962), pp. 120-52.

Discussion of the papers centered on four main points:

1. Science policy in general, including scientific policy planning, government organizations, national research councils, and the machinery for the implementation of science policy
2. Education in science
3. Application of science to development and the role of research
4. Regional cooperation in science and technology.

First Participant: Nigeria had established an Advisory Council for Science and Technology empowered to set up research councils that would develop programs for research in various areas. That the engineering profession was not represented on these bodies indicated that engineers were not considered scientists in certain quarters. This attitude was probably the result of a lack of sufficient understanding of the role of engineering in applied scientific research. A fundamental need in applied scientific research was the establishment of technological standards, particularly in manufacturing. This could be done without engineers. To range farther afield, it was obvious that preventive medicine was not the responsibility of doctors and scientists alone; public-health engineering was indispensable to the application of the findings of doctors, microbiologists, chemists, and others. Meaningful research and application of technological knowledge would have to be a cooperative enterprise engaging the energy and efforts of all kinds of specialists.

Second Participant: The formulation of a science policy presupposed the existence of an economic policy. It was imperative that both be viewed as long-term policies and be related to the country's resources and particularly its manpower. In the formulation of economic policy, all kinds of specialists, including scientists, had a contribution to make, particularly in terms of assessing whether desirable economic objectives were feasible with regard to the existing scientific knowledge and technological capability. In addition, adequate use should be made of indigenous scientific and other expertise, instead of relying on outside technical assistance whenever a scientific or technological problem had to be tackled.

Third Participant: Although the idea of scientific advisory councils had been accepted by most African states, only in a handful

of countries had such bodies been established. This lapse was at-
tributed to the tug of war between government departments for control of these bodies in advance of their establishment. The scientific
advisory council should be independent of all departments and ministries and, ideally, should be under the president or prime minister's
office for budgetary and administrative control. In all other matters,
it should be independent and free from all pressures, particularly
political pressure. Such a body should be broadly based and include
specialists other than scientists, strictly defined. This body, to be
of any use, should possess enough prestige for its recommendations
to be given serious consideration by the government.

Fourth Participant: The liaison between the planning authority
and the science advisory council should be close enough so that
economic objectives and technological possibilities could be matched.
With regard to the composition of the science advisory councils,
"scientist" should not be defined in a restrictive sense to exclude
specialists in nonphysical sciences. Indeed, all specialists concerned
with the problems of development should be represented on the
councils.

Fifth Participant: Viewing the scientific advisory councils on
a national basis could lead to the duplication of activities that might
be wasteful of resources; furthermore, the national basis for scientific
planning, in some instances, would be inadequate for the kind of
scientific activity required. The participants of the symposium
might consider constituting themselves into a group that might play a
larger role, perhaps on a supranational level, in advising on elements
of priorities, exchange, and the certification of scientific credentials
in various fields.

Fourth Participant: In considering the difficulties of determining
the composition of the science advisory council, it was essential
to distinguish between research councils and learned societies.
With regard to a learned society, there should be no difficulty in
deciding who was eligible for membership and who was not. The
society might decide to limit its activities to pure science or engineering, in which case the determination of membership qualifications
was self-evident. A science policy-making body, established to
advise government on aspects of science and technology in development, however, should include a wide range of scientific disciplines,
including the social sciences. It should also include representatives
of appropriate ministries, such as finance and economic planning,
and perhaps those of industry and banking.

Sixth Participant: A scientific advisory council, to be useful,
should establish a set of priorities for scientific and technical research

based on the various surveys of developmental needs. On the basis
of approximate development targets and the rate of progress desired,
the council could make estimates of the manpower and equipment required to implement a given plan. This body could also establish a
register of available scientific and technical personnel so as to reveal
the extent of shortages in various categories and enable the development
of a suitable educational policy for science and technology. Joint
research on a regional basis, as well as the interchange of information
among scientists from contiguous and neighboring countries, should
be encouraged. A most important function of the council would be to
ensure that research and planning undertaken by various government
agencies were compatible with national objectives or otherwise
adapted to meet the needs of the country.

Second Participant: In every country, regardless of size, the
control of the council and the selection of its members would tend
to involve certain political factors that, as had been generally agreed
by the symposium, must be avoided. Countries lacking science
academies could easily use existing professional associations and
other similar bodies to select persons whose competence was assured
and in whom they had confidence. To ensure adequate representation
of the various scientific disciplines, specialist committees could be
set up to be responsible for the development of research programs
within the policy framework of the parent council.

Discussion then moved on to a consideration of the kinds of
research—fundamental, applied, adaptive—that would have the greatest
relevance for African countries.

Seventh Participant: There could be no clear-cut distinction
between applied and fundamental research, since the two were not
mutually exclusive. In the circumstance of most African countries,
it would be difficult to justify research that did not lend itself to
relatively immediate practical application.

Eighth Participant: In Africa, it had been the view that research should be oriented to local problems and that any investment
therein should lead to economic dividends. At the same time, African
scientists, like other scientists, had an interest in the pursuit of
knowledge for its own sake; yet those who provided the funds from
limited resources for research might have an overriding interest
in the solution of specific problems. Added to this was the fact that
one could never tell in advance what practical application could develop from the results of a project of pure or fundamental research.

Second Participant: There need not be any rigid demarcation
line between the research functions assigned to the universities and

those assigned to the research councils. The councils by definition
had a specific national function to perform and should concentrate
on the kind of research applicable to the solution of specific problems.
The universities could divide their energies between the two types
of research as they wished. The main thing was that there be adequate links between the two bodies to ensure the feedback of information.

Seventh Participant: The difference between adaptive and
applied research, while slight, was nevertheless worth mention—
adaptive research being concerned with the modification of borrowed
techniques to the solution of problems in a new environment and
applied research with the search for practical solutions to specific
problems. Furthermore, there was enough useful adaptive research
being carried on in various parts of Africa to make borrowing from
outside unnecessary in many cases. Here, the problem of the
barrier of the two "languages of convenience" was one that African
states should begin to tackle with some urgency.

Ninth Participant: Not only was there an acute shortage of
scientific and technological manpower; those few who had been
adequately trained were being ineffectively used in many countries
because of uncoordinated planning. Highly trained engineers, for
example, might be forced to waste their time on jobs that were the
proper responsibility of the middle-grade technician. Turning to
education, the speaker stated that greater emphasis on the scientific
attitude was needed in the primary and secondary schools, as was a
more practical orientation, so that those not interested in a higher
education might develop a favorable attitude toward working with
their hands. Already the problem was acute, because everybody
wanted a desk job; it was the duty of the educational system to
inculcate into the minds of the young that being "desk-bound" might
not be the acme of achievement.

Eighth Participant: In talking about shortages in scientific
and technological manpower, one needed to know in what categories
and to what extent the shortages occurred and what the needs of the
development plan for these categories of manpower were. Plans
for science education should therefore depend on a manpower survey;
yet there were only a few countries in Africa where such precise
information was available. On another level, because of lack of
guidance and proper counseling, students often went into areas for
which there were no adequate employment outlets—hence, a great
wastage of human and material resources.

Tenth Participant: In regard to the training of available manpower in science and technology, the government could determine

how many bursaries it would give for engineering, how many for medicine, and then relate the number of bursaries to the number of personnel required in various fields. While it could be charged that this method infringed on the right of the individual by forcing him into a line of study or activity for which he might have no interest, it could also be argued that the individual has some obligations to the nation; but, beyond that, no one had the right to expect the state to support him in undertaking a field of study for which the country had no need. As for the infringement of this method on the academic freedom of the university, it should be noted that governments are also entitled to a certain amount of budgetary freedom in achieving national objectives for which they are responsible to all the people.

Fourth Participant: Academic freedom was a much-abused concept. At the university level, academic freedom was an idea that had obviously come to Africa from abroad and tended to impose a conflict between the aims of the university and its role in society. In cases where it was incumbent upon governments to establish and finance universities, it was unrealistic for the university authorities to claim the right to interpret academic freedom solely in their own terms and particularly to claim the right to set above everything else the desire to maintain "centers of learning." One might refer to the situation in Europe or America, whereby the needs of the country were supposed to be automatically provided for by a large variety of persons "each doing his own thing." The function of African universities, in the present state of development, was to produce people capable of doing things that required doing urgently. To this end, there was need for the review and overhaul of the educational system.

Eleventh Participant: One of the problems African universities would increasingly have to face was how to maintain diversity in the search for knowledge and at the same time ensure that the fruits of education would aid development. In other words, should the university continue to be a forum for scholars irrespective of the use to which their knowledge could be put to the benefit of society, or should it be an institution primarily designed for the training of specialists who would directly aid the process of development? The implications of this problem were now being recognized in those places in the universities and within governments where financial decisions were made.

Third Participant: In conducting accurate surveys, Africans would have to rely on their own people, since only they, and not outsiders, could have knowledge of the variables of local conditions. With regard to the training of scientists for the tasks that have to be faced both in science as science and science in relation to development, good science teaching should be available right from the primary school to the university level. A related problem was the so-called self-help schemes of building schools. The result was that, unwittingly, a bias would be created in favor of nonscience-oriented schools. Such an exercise called for an approach that started from scratch, looked at the environment, identified the needs, and worked out ways in which these needs could be met.

Fourth Participant: One difficulty about manpower surveys was that they had to be dependent upon predictions about economic growth, and it was often difficult to make sound predictions in this sector. Manpower surveys were not a panacea for making predictions about future requirements. Industry was still operating in the colonial mold and had not yet been educated to think in terms of people trained in technological institutions. Yet, the use of graduates at lower levels was wasteful of resources and manpower, and employers needed to appreciate this fact.

Twelfth Participant: A great weakness of the educational systems in Africa was the derived attitude toward work. During the colonial era, the pinnacle of achievement was for Africans to be able to sit in an office in some government department and write minutes. The educational system was geared to the production of clerks for the lower levels of the colonial administration and the needs of commerce, and the attitude this kind of training developed still persisted. The speaker wondered whether there were many agricultural graduates in Nigeria today who ran their own farms. In the advanced countries, people from the land took degrees in agriculture and went back to the land, where they probably made more money than that white-collar worker chained to a desk. The problem of maldevelopment of trained manpower was a serious one and could bear further discussion. Some of the effects of this policy were quite bizarre. Thus, it was possible to find a graduate in agriculture teaching scriptures in some secondary school, graduates from business schools employed in jobs other than commerce and industry, and so on—the examples were endless. Manpower surveys and the direction of students toward disciplines that fitted into the national planning objectives could not alone be the solution. What was required was a total change of attitude toward work and a realization that all kinds of work can be satisfying and rewarding if properly pursued.

Tenth Participant: The African's training, wherever possible, was best done in his local environment, not abroad, in order for him to fully appreciate the realities of the African situation. There were many Africans on the faculties of African universities who wished to have their names publicized abroad, irrespective of their standing in Africa; thus, they engaged in research that had little relevance to African problems. Not surprisingly, their students were worse off than those who had studied abroad. One way of securing that university activities be related to the country's problems would be to link them up with research institutes, so that a student doing research in, say, applied chemistry could work partly at the appropriate institute instead of full time at the university. In other words, the practical training aspects of education should be given sufficient emphasis.

Eleventh Participant: Quite apart from the problem of relating education to local problems was that of training those who would impart knowledge within higher educational institutions in the techniques of teaching. It has been assumed, quite erroneously, that a good degree implied the ability to teach, particularly in the university. In Africa particularly, this view had to be rejected and a way found to make the apprenticeship of university lecturers more rigid with reference to the ability and qualification to teach.

Seventh Participant: The fundamental weakness of the African educational system was that it was borrowed from the Middle Ages by way of Britain and France. The tragedy was that, whereas Britain and France had recognized the incompatibility of this type of education to the modern technological world, Africa was hanging on to it as a prized possession. Education was confused with training; thus, the assumption that anyone with a university degree could teach.

Fifth Participant: Similar criticisms of teaching had been expressed in the United States. A manifestation of the student revolution in America was that in every case of faculty promotion in a department, student evaluation of the teacher's competence was given consideration. The importance of certain teaching aids was demonstrated at Berkeley, where students of brain surgery had a television set and a model of the brain in plastic at their disposal. With such aids, a student could go through the process of the operation again and again, so that at the end he might have done the equivalent of dissecting a brain several times. One might also refer to the use in America, as an experiment, of postgraduate training, both for business and for government. This not only had the effect of improving the education level of the people in the business community and the government, but also tended to create an environment in these institutions that was receptive to what the universities wanted to do.

Second Participant: An important role of science in a developing country was to combat prejudices, taboos, and superstition and to make the population at large enlightened about its environment and its capacity to harness the forces of nature for human progress. Science should create confidence in man's ability to use his environment intelligently for his benefit. The popularization of science should thus be one of the objectives of a policy of science education.

Eleventh Participant: It was a misconception that the application of science to development affected only governments. The government was but one agency in society. In modern society, there were other agencies, consisting of individuals, small groups, cooperative societies, firms, and so on; and each of these had the responsibility of applying science as far as possible to the development of its own activities.

Fourth Participant: There was need for dissemination of the results of scientific research in a form that could be readily usable by farmers and others who needed the information. This called for some kind of scientific extension service. In agriculture particularly, this could be a great factor in the upgrading of the productivity of the African farmer.

Third Participant: In spite of many difficulties, these agricultural extension services could be made to work in African countries by imaginative planning and resolute implementation. For example, farmers could be educated to the possibilities of developing by-products from their traditional crops and thereby creating secondary industries.

Fifth Participant: The experiences of other developing countries, such as India and the Philippines, where problems similar to those of Africa had been encountered, could be a useful source of examples in the utilization of semitrained peasantry. Again, oil companies in the Middle East had built up a considerable expertise in these fields, particularly in Saudi Arabia. It would be valuable for a group such as this to reach out not only westward, but to areas that were more comparable in the nature of their problems.

Second Participant: In looking for solutions to the manpower-shortage problem, it was important not to forget the possibility of regional cooperation in the pooling of resources, information, and experience. With regard to the development of specialized training and research institutes, for instance, it made much more sense to establish regional training centers, instead of each African country striving to set up an expensive center for itself.

Third Participant: The fact that a number of universities were operating joint training areas indicated that it might be easier to

to develop these cooperative relationships through informal agreements, rather than through the signing of formal protocols. The
OAU's Scientific Council for Africa was keenly interested in scientific
cooperation, and there was a committee currently investigating the
possibility of establishing a "center of excellence" in mining and
geology.

Ninth Participant: One method of encouraging scientific cooperation in Africa would be the establishment of regional documentation
centers, or even a continental documentation center, under the
auspices of the OAU. These centers would be relatively easy to
establish, not the least of the reasons being that they would not require elaborate formal agreements. Indeed, a number of universities
could agree to begin by exchanging information, and this could lead
naturally to the establishment of a central depository, to which
African research workers would have access.

Fourth Participant: A major obstacle to the development of
cooperation in Africa was the existence of linguistic barriers, which
had been part of Africa's "colonial heritage." These were so insid-
ious as to prevent cooperation even between members of the same
tribe, who might speak the same African language but be on either
side of the "imported linguistic frontier." Such an obstacle could be
removed if the study of English and French were made compulsory
in all African schools.

PART

III

**PRIORITIES
FOR
DEVELOPMENT**

6

AGENDA
FOR
DEVELOPMENT
David Carney

The following five-point agenda is proposed as African "priorities" for development-oriented action in the 1970s:[1]

1. Improvement of the quality of human resources: (a) a rational, scientific approach to the universe, community, and environment; man and his place in society and the world—as well as belief in the ability and desire to change and improve one's environment; (b) investment in science and technology, and especially in a science-oriented system of education and training, with a greater allocation of resources to training (scientific, technical, and professional) as compared with education; (c) a new concept in education and training, emphasizing quality, flexibility, and the optimum use of educational resources, in preference to quantity and fixed conventional ratios in educational input-output relationships; (d) tackling the communications problem by the compulsory adoption of English or French, as the case may be, as a second official language; (e) state-sponsored, as well as intercountry, efforts and joint projects, in respect of the implementation of (a) to (d)

2. An African-oriented system of transportation and communications, ensuring the mobility of persons, ideas, and goods (resources and material capital) within subregional areas in the first instance; the first step toward any meaningful discussion of the internal or domestic market of Africa

3. Rationalization and integration of industrial activity within and between countries, with increasing emphasis on the agro-industrial and regional-planning approach to economic growth, taking due account of the spatial basis of growth and development—that is, the localization element in the implementation of development

4. Subregional cooperation and integration arrangements in the fields of transport, communications, trade and tariffs, money and

banking, and social legislation, assuming the continuation of existing multicountry institutions and arrangements, the extension of their coverage, and their transformation into effective subregional, and eventually regional, institutions.

5. Africa-wide governmental support for a philosophy and a policy of self-reliance, oriented toward Africa and Africans; governmental programs of information and reeducation geared to mental and intellectual decolonization.

What follows is a discussion of some specific matters under each point of this agenda.

HUMAN RESOURCES

As a starting point in the discussion of the first item on the agenda, it may be remarked that the honeymoon with planning in Africa is over, but hopefully there remains a much deeper understanding of the difference between planning and development. In a certain way, Africans, like their economic mentors in Western Europe and America, have been the unsuspecting victims of the theories they embraced. Western economists have taken as their fundamental doctrine of growth and development that growth, and by implication development, proceeds out of land, labor, capital (machines), and organization (management). Having lived in a world in which science and technology exist and their progress is taken for granted, Western economists may be forgiven for making the "concealed assumption" that science and technology exist in Africa and therefore the usual formula for combining the four factors should lead to growth, and thus to development.

In fact, however, this assumption is true of very few countries in Africa. Again, Western economists could go on to assume that those countries in need of scientific and technological know-how could import it in the form of foreign scientific and technical personnel. But, while the former (application of science and technology by others) undoubtedly would lead to growth, only the latter (application by Africans) could lead to African development. In economics, unlike in law, it is unfortunately untrue that "he that does a thing by another, does it himself." The law of agency, or of master and servant, has no counterpart in the science and technology of production.

Education

It is of paramount importance that the improvement in the quality of human resources in Africa take the form of a widespread diffusion of rational and scientific ideas, of formal science education in schools and universities, and of the establishment of laboratories and work-shops for the training of technicians and technologists—primarily in Africa, but without eliminating similar training abroad in specializa-tions that may take time to establish in Africa.

This raises the much-debated question of the transfer of science and technology. It is now over two decades since technical-assistance programs first became established, the most important of which have been those of the United Nations. It was believed that the most impor-tant transfer needed at the time was that of technical know-how, rather than of technical "know-what." Emphasis seems to have been placed overwhelmingly on manipulative or operational skills, to the grave neglect of substantive knowledge, acquired on the spot in a familiar environment and then applied.

Even in the realm of education, the quantitative demand for formal schooling formulated by politicians for their teeming populations has left an unmistakable orientation on the program of UNESCO. The type and quality of education have taken second place to the superficial instruction that passed for education in the past—namely, the literacy tools of reading, writing, and arithmetic. Much of the resources of the organization has thus gone to formal educational and cultural activities, leaving a sad gap in the scientific fields. This balance cannot be redressed unless and until politicians are themselves suffi-ciently educated to recognize the importance of education in science and technology.

This may be regarded by some as asking too much of politicians in contemporary Africa. Perhaps. But there is no other way known of getting development started by the people who want to benefit from its fruits. The sooner this is recognized throughout the length and breadth of Africa, the better it will be, and the less time will be wasted on ineffective complaints, disillusionment, and expectation of miracles. There is no substitute for science, mathematics, and technology in development. Thus, one must consider the possibilities of restructuring the educational systems in Africa in such a way as to turn out development-oriented human resources.

The majority of African countries (almost half of them) spend between 1 and 3 percent of their national incomes on education, another quarter spend 2 to 6 percent, and probably 1 or 2 percent of the coun-tries spend as high as 5 to 10 percent. These statistics are not exclu-sive to Africa, nor is the high percentage of recurrent expenses going to teachers' salaries (60 to 80 percent or more). The range of fluc-tuations of the percentages paid on salaries is much wider in Africa than in Europe, however, where more countries also spend a higher proportion of their national incomes on education than do African countries in general. The biggest spenders among all countries devote 5 to 10 percent of their national incomes to education.

Admittedly, African countries face the problem that most of the 60 to 80 percent of their education budget goes to pay salaries of the hordes of unqualified and untrained teachers—quite apart from the worldwide rise in salary levels. It is also clear that the burden of educational expenditures in Africa, as in other developing (or undeveloped) countries of the world, consists not so much in the percentage of national income spent on this activity (admittedly this could still be raised in many African countries) as in the high percent of the state budget (25 percent or more in most African countries) going to education alone and in the high percent of recurrent educational expenditures going to teachers' salaries, leaving relatively little for teaching materials and equipment.

There is little doubt that increasing the percent of national income spent on education is no solution if the increase is to be shared in the same way as at present or to continue to bulk as large in the incremental, as it does in the total, government budget. Policy prescription in the educational field is therefore to alter the structure and content of education so that more science, mathematics, and technology are included; the proportion of recurrent educational budget spent on teachers' salaries is reduced, while that on materials and equipment is increased; and the proportion of total government budget given over to education decreases, while that of national income increases from, say, 3 to 5 percent, and eventually to 5 to 10 percent.

The inclusion of more science, mathematics, and technology in the educational system is not a simple matter. The introduction of rational scientific ideas into the society at all levels and at all ages is the primary step. There is evidence to indicate that the high percentage of drop-outs from the entire school system in African countries is closely connected with the clash between traditional, nonrational ideas and values, which the child picks up at an early age, and the rational, modern, scientific ideas to which he is later exposed in school. There is very little else so fundamental and pervasive as this clash of ideas to explain the educational malaise of the undeveloped. Following are typical examples of the drop-out rate in the elementary school system in five countries: Algeria, 62.9 percent; Brazil, 64.4 percent; Columbia (rural zones), 96.3 percent; Chad, 81.3 percent; and Sierra Leone, 56 percent.[2]

It seems clear that a system of education that does not suit 55 to 97 percent of the pupils must be, if not wrong, in great conflict with the society itself. Consequently, the ground has to be prepared at all levels of society by the state, using all its resources for mass education, which it now mostly deploys on political propaganda, to sow the seed-bed of modern, rational ideas from which the child could be nourished before the years of formal schooling begin. The cost of this operation would have to be included in the cost of modern education. Fortunately, however, it could be conducted with little additional expense to what the state now spends on information services in many African countries.

A new concept of education will be necessary alongside this operation. The technique of organization and decision-making, coupled with the technical requirements of the modern economy, dictate a pyramidal structure of manpower requirements, in which top-level manpower in the managerial, executive, and professional categories constitutes the apex, followed by a larger group of middle-level manpower (technicians, craftsmen, operatives, and so on) and ending with a broad base of lower-level manpower. In order to reflect this type of manpower distribution, the educational system, duly oriented toward rational and scientific ideas, would provide basic schooling at the elementary level for all the population, the majority of whom will terminate at that level and constitute the lower manpower; comprehensive secondary education, with a wide range of literary, commercial, vocational, and technical possibilities for training those who go through elementary school, a minority of whom will constitute the middle-level manpower; and higher education for a minority of the middle level, who will proceed to qualify for high-level posts in the executive, managerial, and professional categories. Implied in this concept of education is a new concept of democracy—namely, education for all, but to different levels of attainment as required by the dictates of the modern economy.

Social Organization

In order to appreciate the tasks involved in bringing about this transformation of the African economy, one should note that the normal demographic process dictates also a pyramidal population structure, in which the common variable is age, the youngest at the base of the pyramid, the oldest at the apex. In traditional society, as in the typical pyramidal organization, authority resides at the top and flows downward in the form of instructions through various age groups to the foot soldiers of society, the children, who, like good soldiers, do without questioning why.

Because knowledge and authority are equated with age (which assumes a pyramidal structure), social control is automatically demographically determined. "Knowledge" here means "traditional wisdom," based on nonrational, nonscientific (or prescientific) ideas and mythology, the monopoly of which rests at the top, to which all personal responsibility is transferred and which acts as mediator between the individual and society, on the one hand, and the universe of the seen and the unseen, on the other.

The demographic pyramid in traditional society, moreover, is closely associated with a stable manpower structure, in which the traditional rulers and elders, landowners, priests, medicine men, and witch doctors are at the top; a larger group of tradesmen and craftsmen in the middle; and a still-larger group of fishermen, hunters, and peasants at the bottom. Here, there clearly is two different worlds of ideas: the modern, represented by the dynamic science-and-technology-oriented, pyramidal manpower structure of the modern economy; and the traditional or prescientific, represented by the stable demographic-social pyramid. The task of education in African society is therefore one of creating a revolution of ideas that would transform the stable demographic, tradition-bound pyramid into the dynamic, technological, modern pyramid.

The proper utilization of qualified and trained manpower is just as important as its formation. Inefficient use of trained manpower is the practical equivalent of nonexisting trained manpower and ranks high among the development problems of Africa. Elsewhere, the author has stated that contemporary administrative practice in Africa is marked by the following:

1. Inadequate recognition of the need for administrative training

2. The belief that administrative experience increases not by in-depth specialization, but by variety of job experience (i.e., superficiality), combined with the frequent practice of job personalization, instead of delegation of work and responsibility; this implies lack of continuity of experience and operations and the perpetual making of new starts

3. A primitive level of communications and decision-making technology—cumbersome procedure forms, endless meetings by top civil servants, and a record of poor implementation in regard to decisions already taken.[3]

A serious problem is the

current practice of shifting permanent secretaries from one ministry to another, often after years spent in acquiring the necessary expertise or even specialized training relevant to the work of the particular ministry. One of the adverse consequences of this practice is that permanent secretaries are in fact not permanent, and their deputies (where they are not also rotated around) have to accustom themselves to the individual style of operation and management of each new boss. This is not only hard on the deputy (who may have spent a good deal of time and effort being a good backstop to the former boss), as he now has to readjust to the new boss, with grave possibilities of mutual friction and discontent, but the work of the ministry suffers with each changeover.

Moreover, the new boss has to spend a year or more orienting himself to the subject-matter and activities of his new ministry. Consequently, a good deal of time is wasted in a whole series of readjustments, re-learning the job or a new style of working, with grave risks of discontinuity of old policies and activities, and the continual start of new but uncompleted activities. In some cases the rotation of civil service heads may become so frequent that for years nothing seems to get done in any ministry.[4]

What is obviously called for is more stability (less rotation) at the top echelons of the administrative hierarchy—and then allowing rotation only between related jobs—and more rotation at the lower echelons in order to allow for freedom of choice in job selection and development of interests that might not otherwise arise.

It is only in such an environment that it becomes possible for civil service heads to have enough time to follow the progress and growth of their ministries, consider the current allocation and utilization of available manpower, and plan for its better utilization, as well as for on-the-job or other training programs for new staff.[5]

Language

The improvement of communication and sharing of ideas is an important aspect of the development of the quality of human resources. In Africa, this means a vulgarization of the two main languages of communication, French and English. One of the benefits of the colonial era in Africa has been the overall simplification and unification of the linguistic map, in which mostly French and English have replaced the thousands of dialects that impeded communication of ideas across wide areas. This is a factor apt to be overlooked in the general condemnation of the evils of colonialism. This is not meant to imply, however, that linguistic unification is worth all the trials of colonialism. All that is intended is to point out the fact that good and evil are often inextricably intertwined.

Be that as it may, the linguistic picture still leaves much to be desired. Chiefly, the Anglophone-Francophone dichotomy can still be used as an instrument of havoc and neocolonialism by those whose interest lies in keeping the two language groups from coming together in mutual understanding of their common problems and aspirations. The problem is serious enough to merit specific mention in the Pearson Commission report:

> It will take many years for the multiplying effects of educa-tion to change appreciably the proportions of skills in the labor force. This makes it necessary to adapt the organi-zation and content of education very rapidly to the unique needs of different African countries, and particularly to the elimination of language barriers between francophone and anglophone Africa.[6]

It is imperative, therefore, that both French and English be widely adopted in Africa as first and second (or vice versa) official languages, these being the two languages most widely spoken on the continent. If a start was made now in schools and universities, it would take hardly more than a decade for a reasonable degree of bilingualism to become prevalent throughout Africa. African countries can ill afford to play the role of surrogates in whatever cultural or linguistic battles are presumed to be fought between the Gauls and the Anglo-Saxons. Given their own indigenous languages, Africans must regard any foreign languages only as mere tools of communication.

AN AFRICA-ORIENTED SYSTEM OF TRANSPORT AND COMMUNICATIONS

The Colonial Period

The pattern and role of transportation and communications in the colonial period in Africa were conceived in order to promote the economic growth and development of the metropolitan countries by linking the markets of the colonial territories to those of the metro-politan countries—that is, to Europe.

This is clearly seen in the direction of the main roads and railways directly from the coast to the interior, rather than laterally along the coast to connect the countries of Africa. Given the existence of different colonial jurisdictions, this pattern was logical and in-evitable and was aimed to achieve the following objectives:

1. Economic, military and administrative control. In the context of the existing technology, railways were suitable for hauling bulky,

nonperishable raw materials to the coast from the interior—timber and other forest products (cocoa, coffee, and soon), mineral ores (e.g., iron, phosphates, gold and diamonds, chrome ores, and tin). Railways were also suitable for troop movements to the interior and the borders (motor transportation was not in vogue at the start of the colonial period), and roads were constructed as feeders to railways to connect administrative centers.

2. Avoidance of contact with colonial territories under other jurisdictions as well as other monetary zones. Wherever adjacent territories were under the same jurisdiction, these were, of course, linked together—for example, Kenya, Uganda, and Tanganyika after World War I.

The aim here was to isolate different colonial jurisdictions and monetary zones: Gambia was completely isolated from Senegal, forming an enclave along the Gambia River and thereby isolating the Casamance region from the rest of Senegal; the Katanga-Matadi rail line in the Congo (Kinshasa) had to run all the way to the west coast of the continent instead of to the east coast, which was closer and would have promoted speedier exit for the minerals of Katanga; and there were no rail or road links among the countries of the Great Lakes region (Tanganyika was in German hands and could not therefore become an outlet for Zambia [then northern Rhodesia]).

Whatever economic growth took place within each colonial country was thus incidental (growth of towns along main road and rail axes and of economic activity along the coastal zones), the main goal of the transportation network being to promote the economic growth of Europe through its direct link-up (by railway and sea) to the colonial markets.

Given the pattern of traffic—bulky exports to the sea coast and less bulky imports into the interior—the pattern of excess capacity of most African railways on the return journey from the coast was established and became an important cost factor in railway economics, one that could not easily be overcome by railway tariffs when, subsequently, road transportation developed in competition to railways. It should be noted that, originally, the prevailing concept was to construct roads as feeders to railways in order to avoid such competition and to keep the railways in business. This worked only until the railways became a transportation bottleneck, unable to move all the available traffic speedily enough, thus stimulating the construction of parallel roads for motor transportation.

The use of different railway gauges was not entirely accidental and promoted further isolation of colonial jurisdictions, reducing the possibility of a direct link-up among the railways. Even within the same country, separate gauges were used to isolate company activities from other general economic activities (e. g., the Marampa-Pepel rail link was constructed on a guage different from that of the rest of the railways in Sierra Leone).

The undersea cable communications network played the same role as the transportation network, reinforcing jurisdictional isolation and administrative control. All cable links to former French territories passed through Paris, all to former British territories through London. The tariff rates were also discriminatory and designed to reduce communications contact between territories under different colonial jurisdictions.

Other institutional developments that took place in the colonial period also followed naturally the jurisdictional boundaries—monetary zones, for example.

With the development of air transportation, which technically is more flexible than railways and roads, carrier schedules neverthe-less reflected the integral nature of each metropolitan zone. The major objective was to link up countries under each zone—the various airlines in West, East, or Central Africa—rather than according to convenience and regardless of jurisdiction.

The Post-World War II Independence Period

Whereas in the colonial period the main objectives of the African transportation and communications systems were metropolitan growth and development, in the independence period following World War II the objective of African economic growth and development has come to the foreground in discussions. This has certain implications for the restructuring, as well as the modification, of the existing transporta-tion and communications network. Thus, the concept of African eco-nomic integration on a subregional, and eventually regional, basis cuts across the colonial pattern of separate colonial jurisdictions in transportation, communications, trade, and monetary markets. In view of the historical pattern, however, two different trends are discernible: the reinforcing of the colonial pattern of transportation and communications and the attempt to link up the various separate and existing colonial transportation and communications systems. It should be noted that the first is stronger than the second (which has hardly proceeded beyond the blueprint stage) and is still very much intact.

Reinforcing the Colonial Network

From the point of view of the interest of former metropolitan powers, it is obvious that their economic advantages continue to be

served by reinforcing the existing structures of transportation, communications, and trade. This is more evident in the former French zone
than in the former British zone, where the independence period has
resulted in a greater weakening of the colonial links.

The concept of "Eurafrique," or the association of the former
French colonies with the European Economic Community (EEC), is not
a new development, but the strengthening of a preexisting system based
on the concept of transportation- and communications-oriented spheres
of influence. The only new factor is that former colonial powers of
Africa, with the exception of the British, have given up the concept of
competition for that of cooperation in their economic relationships
with their former colonies. This is inevitable, since the only colonial
power of any influence in Africa, again with the exception of the British,
are the French; the Belgians, Germans, and Italians have practically
lost their former territories, while the Portuguese and Spaniards have
a shaky hold on theirs. This development explains the dominance of
France in the EEC, as well as the conflict between France and Britain
over the latter.

Britain, having lost a good deal of the economic foothold it had
in its former African colonies, works on the assumption that it is too
late to regain those links and maintain them as the French still do—
hence, its attempts to join the EEC, which, from the viewpoint of all
former metropolitan countries, would be more to their interest. This
would complete the cooperative arrangement and extend the field to
take in the former British colonies and consolidate the preexisting
pattern of metropolitan-colonial economic relations.

France, however, takes the opposite view, still regarding
Britain as a powerful competitor whose bargaining position would be
strong if it entered the EEC with such links as remain with its former
colonies. The strategy of France is therefore to establish, where
possible, direct economic links with the former British colonies by
way of trade and investment, a strategy that is being assisted by the
seeking of direct contacts with the EEC by Nigeria and East Africa.
This strategy reveals itself in French investment interests and technical assistance projects in East Africa (Tanzania and Zambia, especially), in Sierra Leone (harbor construction and water supplies),
and in eastern Nigeria (oil deposits), which explains the alignment
of British support with the federal government and of the support of
France and its former colonies—Gabon and the Ivory Coast—for
Biafra in the thirty-month conflict between the Nigerian Federal
Government and eastern Nigeria.

French and EEC investments through the European Development
Fund are concentrated on maintaining the existing transportation and
communications network in the eighteen associated countries of Africa.
Railways are being modernized, extended, and reinforced. New roads

are being constructed to reinforce the existing pattern, with emphasis
on separate national road systems rather than on subregional roads.
The previous telecommunications system in francophone Africa is
being consolidated through the Union of Africa and Malagasi Posts and
Telecommunications, the airline system through Air Afrique and Union
de Transportes Aeriens. In former British West Africa, the previously
defunct West African Airways Corporation airline is being restored,
with Ghana and Nigeria as the major partners, and the East African
Airways system remains intact.

Resistance to linking up these and other existing systems into a
regional pattern is being encountered in the form of selective granting
or nongranting of landing rights. Thus, Ethiopian Airlines finds it
difficult to extend its run along the West African coast up to Senegal,
and there are problems between the East African and Nigerian airlines.

Telecommunications are still being kept separate and intact as
between anglophone and francophone Africa. The cable systems of
Francophone and Anglophone Africa still converge on Paris and London,
respectively, and discriminatory tariff rates still keep the two systems
separate.

Former colonial countries, chiefly British and French, continue
to find it easier to establish contact with London and Paris than with
one another through the orientation of the existing communications
and airlines, supplemented in the case of air transportation by Air
France and British United Airways.

One serious consequence of this reinforcing of the colonial
pattern of communications and transportation is a communications
blackout whenever a disruption of traffic occurs at the metropolitan
end in Paris or London and a transmission of higher costs in imports
from the metropolitan countries, which are still the main suppliers.

The Attempt to Link Up Systems

In spite of the trend toward the reinforcing of the existing colonial transportation and communications network, it is recognized
widely among African countries that growth and development in Africa
can be served as a major objective only by modifying the pattern
through interconnections and by establishing new links. Thus, the
question of subregional integration in Africa becomes basically a
transportation and communications problem. The comparative futility
of all subregional integration movements so far, with the exception
of the integration movement between Kenya, Uganda, and Tanzania,
is a result of the apparent unwillingness to accept this fact.

In this light, the proposed subregional transportation links in West, East, Central, and North Africa assume significance and are seen to be the keys to any subregional integrative movement, which is unlikely to get off the ground without them, and will remain little more than pious wishes. Railroads are unlikely to play a significant part in this development, as compared with motor roads and air transportation, given the expense and rigidity of rail routes and their primary suitability for bulky goods.

The proposed transportation link between North and West Africa from Algeria to Mali and Niger is being delayed by an irrelevant technical issue of motor road versus railway and by indecision over a French proposal to construct a railway instead of the two motor-road links under consideration. The clear superiority of motor roads over railroads is indicated by the following considerations in their favor: they are relatively cheaper to construct as a network; there is greater flexibility in regard to the rolling stock that uses motor roads; the transportation of oil and gas by railways, which should justify their construction in the desert area, is made irrelevant through the cheaper construction and maintenance of pipelines; current technology enables motor transportation to adapt itself to rough terrain and rough desert roads through construction of special tires and caterpillar wheels; and efficient rail transportation would require electrification, an additional expense.

Concerning the East African transport link, a major step is being taken by the Tanzania-Zambia railway, for which financing has been proposed by the African Development Bank and the People's Republic of China. Motor roads, however, are likely to be cheaper and more flexible than a railway and to make a great contribution to the economic development of the subregion.

The West African road transport system is being delayed unduly for reasons unconnected with the economics of the system. The countries involved seem unwilling to take their major arterial roads up to their borders, and the West African Transportation Authority, based in Monrovia, is practically dead.

It is ironical that in April, 1968, a meeting scheduled for the fourteen countries of the West African subregion, attended by the heads of states and governments of about eight, established a protocol for a West African Economic Community. So long as the transportation problem is ignored, the West African Economic Community, like the West African Free Trade Area, the West African Customs Union, the Central African Customs Union, or the Union of States of Central Africa are likely to remain little more than still-born organizations.

The Central African transport system is mostly at the blueprint stage, aimed at developing a rational system of roads and railways.

The African Telecommunications Plan

As a joint program by the ECA and the International Telecommunications Union (ITU), the plan for a Pan-African telecommunications system was discussed in 1960 by the Subcommittee for Africa at the First Planning Assembly of the International Consultative Committee for Telephony and Telegraphy of the ITU. The so-called Dakar Plan was established by the subcommittee at its meeting in Dakar in 1962. The plan calls for a new network, linking African countries two by two by direct circuits or by suitable traffic-concentration points; the wide use of overhead wire lines, supplemented by radio relay links and submarine cables; the extension of the present high-frequency radio system to fill the gap until the new plan is implemented, which requires an interim crash program to provide telephone and telegraph services between African capitals via high-frequency radio in order to fill the present communications gap between and among these capitals; and a long-term goal to provide quick, reliable, and cheap communications to all parts of Africa and between any part of Africa to all parts of the world and vice versa. The last objective, taking into account the great size of Africa, has led to examination of the possibility of communications by satellites.

This plan is still "at the plan stage." There is evidence of a degree of hesitation—if not reluctance—on the part of ITU to proceed with it, considerations of expense aside. Naturally, such a plan would take many years to implement. The essential thing is that a beginning should be made.

Obstacles

Obstacles to the implementation of a transportation and communications system oriented to growth and development in Africa include the following:

1. Presumed cultural differences and ideas: Francophone and Anglophone.

2. Neglect of the common condition: the common denominator of tribal social structure, common needs and aspirations.

3. Support of existing colonial structures in transportation, communications, and monetary zones.

4. Presumed fears of political domination of one African country by another.

5. Preference for supporting foreign economies, rather than the economy of any African country.

6. Internal and external financial and other forms of resistance to the implementation of projects designed to promote economic integration and growth at the level of transportation and communications.

7. Inadequate thought and recognition by African governments and leaders of the basic necessity of a new transportation and communications structure to African economic growth.

RATIONALIZATION AND INTEGRATION OF INDUSTRIAL ACTIVITY

Increasing emphasis is being placed on the regionalization of development, chiefly the spatial location of projects and their interrelationship with other projects of a complementary nature in agriculture, industry, and services, both within and between countries. Starting with the location aspect, development has to proceed, as always, from the ground up—i. e. , on the basis of the available human and material resources. One of the handicaps to African development, in this respect, is not only inadequate basic knowledge of the location and volume of specific mineral resources, but also the exportation abroad of whatever minerals are currently under exploitation. If Africa is to develop on the basis of its material resources, it is imperative that the resource base be oriented toward domestic use.

A preliminary step in this direction would be the convocation of an African Conference of Ministers of Mines, under the auspices of the Organization of African Unity (OAU), to discuss existing mining agreements and concessions, exchange experiences on the working of these agreements, the allocation of benefits, and the impact of such agreements not only on the general economy of mineral-rich countries, but also on the manpower position. This last point is relevant in that foreign exploitation of minerals in Africa is a direct result of the absence of African manpower with technical knowledge and experience in the mining field. It should be interesting, therefore, to see the progress made in the training of African geologists and mineralogists for purposes of utilizing mineral resources locally. Of similar interest would be a discussion of experiences with nationalization vis-à-vis other arrangements for exploitation and control of mineral resources.

In regard to industries already established under various incentive schemes giving priority to import-substitution industries, it is important to note that the insertion and integration of a new project into the existing industrial network has never been given much consideration. As a result, the industries implanted under such incentives exist on an individual basis, without the economic links that generate good business and income multiplication.

This consequence is a direct reflection of the weaknesses of the method of project evaluation generally adopted in planning bureaus in Africa. Projects are examined one at a time, instead of each being taken as one in a group or package of related projects. The plain fact is that the establishment of projects is a task for private enterprise in most African countries. Consequently, the examination of projects proposed by private enterprise is done less from the viewpoint of the technical and direct, as well as indirect, effects on the economy than from the necessity to decide whether or not to extend pioneer or incentive privileges to the projects' sponsors in accordance with an official list of preferred industries.

The achievement of integrative planning and implementation of industrial projects lies in the following three-pronged approach:[7]

1. The planning and evaluating team must be composed of experts in various technical and economic fields who together examine each individual project set before them, whether it concerns the construction of a rubber factory, a school, or a clinic.

2. Development plans should be conceived and built around projects that are complementary in execution; hence, they must be examined and evaluated separately as well as together.

3. Implementation of projects should take the form of locating composite project packages in geographic space (regions), with consideration being given to the interdependence of regions through the intercomplementarity of regional-project packages.

Thus, integrative planning, an approach that cuts across sectors, is composed of the following elements: complementarity of projects; the project packages; the collective evaluation of projects, separately and in a package; and the strategic location of projects in the package or plan among new or already existing projects. It is, ideally, the regional-planning approach.[8]

One interesting application of this approach lies in the area of economic community arrangements or the establishment of common markets. The conventional approach to this problem runs in terms of the necessity to allocate industries among countries in such a way as to distribute, fairly, the benefits, as well as the costs. It is here submitted that a satisfactory solution cannot be obtained along those lines, since the approach overlooks the necessity for integration of the activities of all the member countries of the market. And this integration cannot be achieved if entire industries are allocated to particular countries, since the benefits will accrue only to the beneficiary country, and it could be difficult to find enough industries to go around fairly. Rather, one should think in terms of allocating different stages of the industry to the different countries, thus automatically integrating the factors markets of all the participating countries. This also automatically builds up goodwill in all member countries and secures their markets for the final products. Thus, the rule for integrating common markets is: allocate processes of each industry, not entire industries, to individual members of the market.

The objection that this procedure could lead to a sacrifice of economies of vertical integration in one country by seeking to secure vertical integration over the economic space of several countries, account being taken of increased transportation costs, can be disposed of as follows.

First, in a common market, the advantages of integration of factors and products markets are worth paying the price of an extra increase in transport costs, if the alternative is a sacrifice of the markets of some of the member countries of the market area. Second, in the context of a common market, the true transport costs and other costs of production are those of the market area as a whole, rather than those of a particular member country, be it the cheapest. Last, if the increase in transport costs makes products less competitive with similar imports, it is easier to impose the cost of protection of the market in terms of increased product prices when the incomes and employment of all member countries are at common risk.

It seems time that this new approach to the industry-allocation problems of common markets be given a trial, as it contains the possibility of a breakthrough in this particular field.

SUBREGIONAL COOPERATION AND INTEGRATION ARRANGEMENTS

If Africa had the scientific, mathematical, and technological know-how and "know-what" today, as well as an Africa-oriented system of transportation and communications, industrial rationalization, and integration, it would still find its development handicapped by trade and tariff barriers and by nonintegrated money and banking systems. These are the institutional barriers that keep inter-African trade down to 5 percent or less of the total value of the external trade of African countries.

With tariff systems mutually discriminatory among the existing monetary zones still largely in vogue since the colonial era, African countries are painfully but slowly dismantling the trade barriers among them. Several bilateral agreements have been signed between countries belonging to different monetary zones, but these are difficult to operate, even by agreement between central banks to compensate payments, chiefly because of the external monetary and exchange controls imposed by the former metropolitan countries that still regulate their currencies.

The inauguration of the Association of African Central Banks toward the end of 1969 is a good sign that African countries will finally address themselves to the problems of money and banking that bedevil their exchanges within the continent. This is fortunate, because it leads the way to the realization that trade and tariff revisions among the African countries themselves is of equal importance with trade and tariff revisions between African countries, on the one hand, and the industrialized countries, on the other.

An African Conference on Money and Banking, Trade and Development (COMBTAD), is an urgent "priority," long overdue. This might be arranged under the umbrella of the OAU.

> It is often argued that there could not be much trade among various African countries because they produce mostly the same basic raw materials, which they could not process, but have to sell abroad. While this argument is quite sound from the theoretical point of view, it ignores the fact that, already, quite a lot of import-substituting enterprises have been established in various African countries, some similar, others showing a wide range of differences. Indeed, the same people who argue that there cannot be trade between countries producing the same raw materials now find themselves arguing that there cannot be trade between countries producing the same manufactured goods. Apart from the error in the argument, how about those cases where countries produce different manufactured goods, or where manufactured goods could be exchanged for raw produce?

> There have been several cases in recent years where one African country refuses to conclude a trade agreement with another, involving the exchange of peanuts for

manufactured goods. The peanut producer preferred to use up its foreign exchange importing the same type of goods from abroad. The advantage of increasing exchanges among African countries, wherever possible, is that they save scarce foreign exchange, which they now spend importing similar goods from abroad. And the scope of such possible exchanges is widening every day.

The recent Small Industries Exhibition mounted by the United Nations Economic Commission for Africa on the occasion of the Ninth Session of the Commission and its tenth anniversary was somewhat of an eye opener (February 1969). Indeed, in many cases the term "small industries" was a misnomer. But even without this exhibition one could enumerate many cases where profitable trade could take place: meat and dairy products from Kenya to non-meat producing countries of Africa in exchange for, say, textiles or processed cocoa; manufactures like textiles and hardware from North Africa to sub-Saharan Africa in exchange for peanuts, cashew nuts, rice, etc. Indeed, if the African countries took the matter into serious consideration, they could easily have called a trade conference in Africa, instead of in Geneva or New Delhi, to examine what possibilities of exchange already exist among them.

This is a very elementary matter and the fact that it has not been considered or implemented before now is an indication that the African countries may not be sufficiently aware of where to start or where their problems really lie. It has become so fashionable to look outside Africa for the cause of African problems that problems of patently local origin have to be projected externally in order to be recognized.

One of the fallacies commonly heard is the statement that so long as African countries maintain currencies that are convertible or—which is more often the case—based on convertible currencies, like the pound sterling or the franc, existing monetary arrangements present no handicap to a wider exchange among the various African countries. What this false argument always refuses to take into account, or explain, is why African countries should ever use foreign currencies or assets in foreign exchange—whether of unlimited convertibility or not is irrelevant—to settle what are purely domestic exchanges within the continent. Foreign exchange remains

scarce for all African countries, whether their currencies
are based on it or not, and it makes no sense whatsoever—
indeed, it is a waste of resources—to use it in settling indebtedness among African countries. This is the fundamental argument for payments agreements among African
countries, which no amount of unlimited convertibility of
the basic currency can alter or weaken.

So long as the trade and monetary problems remain
unsolved, Africa will continue to face the ironical situation, which is now becoming more widespread, in which
development of manufacturing industries is premised on
the existence of foreign markets. (Such is the case, for
example, in East Africa today.)

This is a reenacting of nineteenth-century economic
colonialism in reverse, without the African countries possessing the political or military power which would give
them effective control over the markets of the developed
countries. Europe industrialized to a large extent on the
raw materials and markets of the tropical countries. But
the situation cannot easily be reversed to enable the tropical countries, now independent, to industrialize on the
basis of the raw materials and markets of Europe. Africa
will have to learn to turn homeward—before it becomes
too late.[9]

And in looking homeward, the first step would have to be the
calling of the proposed COMBTAD conference under the aegis of the
OAU, assembling African ministers of trade, industry, finance, and
development with their advisers to survey the field for cooperation in
trade, money, banking, industrial-incentive legislation, capital transfers, tax legislation, and social legislation. Such a conference would,
naturally, have to set up the appropriate working groups of experts
to examine and prepare detailed programs of action to be implemented
by governmental agencies and central, commercial, and industrial
banks. Needless to add, the conference, as well as its technical working
groups, would have to be established on a permanent basis within the
framework of the OAU in order to yield useful and continuing results.

AN AFRICAN PHILOSOPHY AND POLICY
OF SELF-RELIANCE

There is an unfortunate tendency for outsiders (non-Africans) to
worry over and misinterpret any call to self-reliance. They automatically jump to the false conclusion that this means getting rid of all

foreigners, autarchy, and other nightmares. They overlook the simple fact that the economies of various countries are becoming increasingly interdependent, and rightly and inevitably so. But they also overlook the equally simple fact that Africa can be developed only by Africans, not by foreigners. All that foreigners can contribute is growth, not development.

The primary concern here, however, is with the attitude of Africans toward themselves, their countries, and their continent. It concerns the degree of their mental, emotional, and spiritual commitment to Africa, their desire to effect change and to make the sacrifices involved for the benefit of both themselves and their posterity.

The matter of giving priority to Africa by Africans, the development of a philosophy of "Africa first" (rather than the former metropolitan country) is not going to be easy. It will involve passing through a period of intellectual and mental decolonization, getting rid of the opium and the automatic reflexes of colonialism, developing faith in themselves (without which there cannot be personal dignity), and being willing to assume their own burdens and responsibilities. All this at the same time they need to orientate their thinking along rational, scientific lines! This is a task more difficult than winning political independence; it means no less than an intellectual and spiritual renaissance (or revolution).

If, therefore, one asks why African countries have taken nearly two decades to discover the difference between growth (increased output stimulated by non-Africans) and development (increased output and structural and intellectual change stimulated by Africans), why Africa is only painfully and slowly learning that salvation comes from within, not from without, and why the appropriate agenda for development is overlooked or not included in development plans, the answer is simple: Africans have yet to discover themselves and the world around them.

For some countries, it is a veritable search for identity (not the same thing as the old "African personality," which is merely a political image or presence), a quest to discover whether the African can surrender his thinking, his culture, his hopes and aspirations to another and still remain African. For others, it is a lengthening quest to discover the talents and capabilities of their own people. For all, it is, at the moment, a first timid step toward the assumption of full intellectual and spiritual independence and responsibility. The development of Africa will begin only with the spiritual rebirth of the African people.

NOTES

1. David Carney, "African Development in the 1980's," F. S. Arkhurst, ed., Africa in the Seventies and Eighties: Issues in Development (New York: Praeger, 1970).

2. Figures for all countries, except Sierra Leone, were taken from Le Monde, July 8, 1970, p. 10. Figure for Sierra Leone was taken from the Report of the Commission on Higher Education, (Freetown: February, 1970), p. 5.

3. David Carney, "Utilization of Trained Manpower," in Training Course in Human Resources Planning in Africa, Dakar-Senegal, 6-14 October, 1969 (Addis Ababa: United Nations Economic Commission for Africa, May, 1970).

4. Ibid.

5. Ibid.

6. Partners in Development, Report of the Commission on International Development (New York: Praeger, 1969), p. 278 (emphasis added).

7. See David Carney, "The Integration of Health Planning (Social Planning) with Overall Planning," IDEP/REPRODUCTION/167, April, 1970 (mimeographed).

8. Ibid.

9. Carney, "African Development in the 1980's."

7

**REGIONAL
ECONOMIC
DEVELOPMENT
IN AFRICA**
Samuel A. Aluko

INTRODUCTION

The term "region," when considering regional economic integration and development, is generally used to correspond to the group of countries in an area covered by an economic commission of the U.N. Thus, the major world economic regions are those covered by the economic commissions for Europe, Latin America, Asia and the Far East, and Africa. The region, in each case, tends to be coterminous with the continent. When effective regional economic development problems and prospects are discussed, however, they are done so in terms of the identifiable economic subregions into which the region is divided. In Africa, for instance, the ECA recognizes five subregions:

1. North Africa, consisting of Algeria, Libya, Morocco, Sudan, Tunisia, and the U.A.R. (population, 78.5 million)

2. West Africa, consisting of Dahomey, Gambia, Ghana, Guinea, Ivory Coast, Liberia, Mali, Mauritania, Niger, Nigeria, Portuguese Guinea, Senegal, Sierra Leone, Spanish Sahara, Togo, and Upper Volta (population, 103 million)

3. Central (or Equatorial) Africa, consisting of Angola, Burundi, Cameroon, Central African Republic, Congo (Brazzaville), Congo (Kinshasa), Gabon, Equatorial Guinea, Ruwanda, and Chad (population, 40 million)

4. East Africa, consisting of Botswana, Ethiopia, Kenya, Lesotho, Madagascar, Malawi, Mauritius, Mozambique, Reunion, Somalia, Swaziland, Tanzania, Uganda, and Zambia (population, 81 million)

119

5. South Africa and southern Rhodesia (population, 23.5 million). [1]

The necessity for regional economic integration as a means of promoting more rapid industrial and technological development in Africa is now widely accepted by most African countries and their political and intellectual leaders. The original motivating force for continental union and integration was supplied by the Pan-Africanists. Although the Pan-African ideology has fired little imagination other than at a purely intellectual and visionary level, attempts toward economic integration in both the developed and the developing countries outside Africa—such as the EEC, the European Free Trade Area (EFTA), the Organization of American States (OAS), the Central American Common Market (CACM), the Latin American Free Trade Association (LAFTA), the Caribbean Free Trade Area (CFTA), and the Arab Common Market (ACM), to mention only a few—have given rise to the concern for a more urgent, realistic, and effective economic and political integration as a means of promoting economic growth and political independence. Since many African countries are too small and their economies too fragile for individual achievement of these goals, there is need for cooperation with other neighboring African countries. Even the larger states, like Nigeria, the U.A.R., the Sudan, or the Congo (Kinshasa), have found that this kind of cooperation offers unlimited national economic advantages. [2]

The OAU, which was created in 1963, established an economic and social commission to set up a free-trade area among member states; to harmonize national development plans, particularly in transport and communications, by land, sea, and air; to study the problems of payments agreements between African countries until the establishment of an African payment and clearing union; to standardize a common external tariff among member states; and to set up a monetary zone and a central bank. It was their plan to achieve most of these objectives by cooperating actively with the ECA. At the subregional level, within the French-speaking African countries, there have been and still are organizations of this kind: for example, the West African Customs Union, founded in 1959 by Dahomey, the Ivory Coast, Mauretania, Nigeria, Senegal, Mali, and the Upper Volta (population, 26.3 million); the Equatorial Customs Union, established in 1960 by the Congo (Brazzaville), Cameroon, Gabon, Chad, and the Central African Republic (population, 11.8 million); and the entente set up in 1965 by the Ivory Coast, the Upper Volta, Niger, Dahomey, and Togo (population, 16.8 million). These economic and political groupings have objectives of creating customs unions, redistributing revenue to support poorer members, and harmonizing development plans.

In 1964, proposals were put forward for the establishment of a West African Free Trade Area, to include the Ivory Coast, Guinea,

Liberia, and Sierra Leone (population, 11.2 million). The four countries have set up an Organization for West African Economic Cooperation in Sierra Leone. The Maghreb countries of Morocco, Tunisia, Algeria, and Libya have taken measures, since 1964, to create a customs union to harmonize trade policy and development plans, coordinate tourism, market agricultural products, and establish an iron and steel plant. The U.A.R. and the Sudan are contemplating joining the Maghreb union (population, 78.5 million). In May, 1966, Ethiopia, Kenya, Malawi, Mauritius, Tanzania, and Zambia (population, 54.5 million) signed articles for an Association for an East African Economic Community. The articles for an Association for a West African Economic Community, consisting of Nigeria, Ghana, Liberia, Sierra Leone, Gambia, Senegal, and Togo (population, 79.6 million), were considered in Niamey in October, 1966, and at Accra in April-May, 1967, while the South African Customs Union dates back to 1889 and consists of the Republic of South Africa, Lesotho, Botswana, and Swaziland (population, 20.6 million).

Some countries at present participate in two or more unions, which are regarded as mere talking platforms. More permanent and effective unions will have to be better defined geographically, with each country deciding which union to join in its own subregion.

THE CASE FOR ECONOMIC INTEGRATION

While there is general agreement on the advantages of integration, there is much controversy as to the nature and degree considered desirable. The disagreements occur because of the differences arising from national and sectional particularism, economic and political ideologies, and appraisals of the effects and gains derivable from integration. [3] With reference to the developing countries in general and Africa in particular, economic integration facilitates the achievement of economies of scale, rationalizes location and relocation of production units and encourages specialization in production, enhances industrial efficiency, reduces external vulnerability and dependence of the associated economies, increases the bargaining power of the economies via-á-vis the rest of the world, accelerates the flow of intraunion services and contact with and knowledge of one another, promotes the flow of investment intraregionally and from abroad, and prepares the ground for an ultimate political union. [4]

Economies of Scale

The diversification of the economies of the African countries by means of industrialization and modernization of agriculture is indispensable if they are to redress the unfavorable balance of trade for their traditional exports and meet the ever-rising needs of their peoples. Efficient industrial production requires an optimum market size, because unless the volume of sales reaches a certain minimum, the unit-cost and consequently the consumer-price level will be high and the ability to compete with more efficiently produced goods and services will be low. Production costs in many industries using modern production techniques decline as output increases. Even though a few activities can be efficiently carried on within the narrow confines of individual countries, in view of the large number of small states in Africa and of the very low purchasing power of the people, the individual domestic market is too limited to permit them to reap the full benefit of the economies of scale. Large markets are particularly essential for the production of such goods as iron and steel, nonferrous metals, heavy chemicals, fertilizers, pulp and paper, industrial and farm machinery, electrical equipment, transport equipment, textiles, and durable consumer goods.

It has been calculated, for instance, that between 30 and 50 percent of capital investment could be saved in Latin America if regionally integrated production of most of these goods were to replace the existing nationally determined production units.[5] Were Africa to adopt such an approach to production, for example, similar savings would be possible.[6] The economies of scale take on added importance today because the optimum size of most manufacturing plants is increasing with technological progress, and the areas of success available for small units are diminishing. Therefore, projects not economically feasible or feasible at prohibitive costs become profitable only if undertaken jointly by several countries. Those developing countries that have made the greatest industrial advance are almost exclusively those that possess large internal markets or enjoy easy access to large foreign markets.

Location, Specialization, and Efficiency

Adam Smith has rightly said that division of labor is limited by the extent of the market. Economic policies at the national autarchic level often lead to the establishment of industries without regard to specialization possibilities that exist within an economic region. If, however, industrial planning takes place within a regional or subregional framework, the advantages of specialization are obviously much larger than in one country. This is the more so in the production of industrial goods, such as chemicals, aluminum, paper, automobiles, and machinery, where raw materials and energy costs are significant. If each country in the region or subregion were to specialize in the production of those goods for which it offers comparative advantages, costs would be greatly reduced. A wider market, by permitting specialization, increases and sustains efficient production units in a greater number of establishments. These units will be better able to compete with similar outside units and thus require less domestic tariff protection, under which many industries in the developing coun- tries hide their inefficiency and waste.

In a situation where absolute protection from outside competition exists, internal firms tend to be complacent in management and tech- niques, whereas the existence of other competitors or the inflow of imports from other countries tend to stimulate a spirit of initiative and a search for new ways of improving production for the domestic consumer. In many developing countries today, domestically produced goods under various tariff barriers and incentive concessions are much more costly to the domestic consumer than imported goods. Even though a reasonable degree of protection against the influx and dumping of goods from the developed countries is necessary in order to give domestic investors certainty about the future and to attract foreign investors, the protection ought to be so organized, possibly regionally, that the opportunities of achieving economies of scale, specialization, and operational efficiency are not sacrificed.

Reduction of External Vulnerability

As long as the trading channels of the African countries remain almost exclusively tied to the developed countries, the former are bound to be at the mercy of the trading policies of the latter. This is more so if the African countries remain essentially agricultural and mining exporting countries, many of which depend on single or only a few primary export products. With integration, these countries will be capable not only of diversifying their exports, but also of changing the direction of their external trade relations. They will trade more with one another and export more to other developing countries outside the region or subregion, and such increased trade will thus enhance their capacity to resist the outside shocks generally associated with primary goods-producing countries. Also, the balance- of-payments position of the region will improve, and the freedom of action of the individual countries within the region will be strengthened with less dependence on the more-developed countries. [7]

Increased Bargaining Power

The ineffectiveness of the large number of developing countries of Africa, Asia, and Latin America on the bargaining table with the few rich and powerful developed countries of Europe and North America at the United Nations Conference on Trade and Development (UNCTAD) conferences on the stabilization of the prices of key primary goods aptly demonstrates the fact that the defense of a country or a region's commercial and economic interests depends not only on persuasion, but also on the extent to which the country or region is a major supplier of essential products, on its import potential, and on its ability to meet its import needs by converting primary goods hitherto exported into industrial goods produced at home. The African countries, at present, possess little bargaining power of this kind. But if many of them, continentally or subregionally, were able to combine their import, export, and production potentials, they could conceivably secure better considerations at the UNCTAD negotiations.

The larger the trading area that is negotiating as a single unit, the better the commercial policy treatment it can hope to exact from the outside world and the better its terms of trade. This is the more important, particularly when even the individually powerful developed countries are grouping themselves into larger units so as to increase their superior bargaining strength. Once internal cohesion in the form of merged national markets and joint efforts in foreign-trade policy is achieved, external effectiveness will be greatly enhanced.

Intraunion Flow of Services and Contacts

Intra-African imports today amount to only about 9 percent and exports to about 17 percent of the total African trade, as compared with intra-European imports of about 85 percent and exports of about 66 percent,[8] The largest volume of intra-African imports are by Rhodesia and Malawi, South Africa, Algeria, the Congo (Kinshasa), French West Africa, Morocco, and the Sudan. Such trade is negligible in Nigeria (representing about 1 percent of the value of its imports), Sierra Leone (3 percent), the U.A.R. (3.7 percent), and Ghana (5 percent). Intra-African exports are mostly from South Africa (22.6 percent of its export trade), Rhodesia and Malawi (18.1 percent), Mozambique (13.7 percent), Morocco (12.1 percent), French West Africa (12.6 percent), French Equatorial Africa (11.3 percent), and the Sudan (11.2 percent). Such exports are negligible in Nigeria (1.6 percent), Ghana (4 percent), Sierra Leone (5 percent), and the U.A.R. (5 percent).[9]

Intra-African trade and commercial contacts are made minimal as a result not only of the illegal border trade across unpoliced or inadequately policed land boundaries and the restriction of trade with the apartheid regions of South Africa and Rhodesia, but also of the inadequacy of transport and communications. It is easier and quicker to reach Europe or America from most capitals of African countries than to reach even nearby African countries. Intra-African travel and tourism are reduced to a minimum, the effect being that even highly educated Africans are more at home in Europe and America and know more of the history and problems of those continents than they do of their own. Economic union is designed to reverse these trends. The existing African transportation and communications systems, mainly designed to link individual African countries with the former metropolitan capitals, must be replaced by efficient networks if the much-needed contacts with and knowledge of African countries are to be encouraged among African leaders, scholars, and business-men.

Increased Flow of Investment

Three broad categories of African countries are discernible with respect to financing of domestic investment. First, there are those that depend largely on internal savings, but that have so run down their external reserves as to be greatly in debt. These include Nigeria, Ghana, and other sterling countries in East and Central Africa, the U.A.R., and most of the Maghreb countries. Second, there are those dependent on large foreign investment as the main prop to their econ-omies, such as Liberia, Mauretania, and the majority of the French African countries. The economies of these countries are, so to speak, dominated and controlled by the metropolitan powers that provide the capital. Third, there are those that receive heavy inflow of public funds, but that also suffer from equally heavy outflow of capital in the form of remittances abroad on private accounts of foreign capitalists, usually engaged in mining and manufactures. These include Libya, Zambia, Sierra Leone, the Congo (Kinshasa), and, to some extent, Nigeria. [10] In each of the three cases, the influence of the foreign private and public investors has increased, is increasing, but should be diminished.

To date, too much of the foreign borrowing and foreign invest-ment in Africa has been left to the play of the market forces and gives rise to the playing of one African country against another, reminiscent of the situation with the six Australian states before they established the Loan Council in 1927. A few countries have taken individual actions to limit, control, or nationalize such investments; regional integration, however, will have the effect of encouraging joint action in the granting of incentives, in establishing priorities, in avoiding the duplication of investment in the integrated area, as a means of ensuring that the participation of foreign capital is compatible with the need to strengthen domestic enterprise and that it is absorbed in such a way that the region maintains control over basic activities. It is also likely that by widening the market, encouraging specialization, and improving efficiency, regional integration will attract the necessary foreign

capital in much larger quantum than exists at present. Domestic
capital itself is likely to be increased and to flow to areas of greater
productivity than is possible if the market remains small and national
rather than regional or subregional. 11

Ultimate Political Union

The experiences from other developed and developing countries
tend to show that political integration of a number of separate and
independent countries is likely to be achieved if strong economic links
are forged among them. Furthermore, such an economic organization
is likely to be subject to less disruption owing to political disputes.
Even though it is difficult to delineate where economics ends and
politics begins, the EEC countries and the CACM, both of which include politically aligned and neutral countries, provide examples of
the advantages of separating economic from political cooperation.
The EEC countries, for instance, have, over the years, set up a
Council of Europe, a European Assembly, and a European Court.
Where there is a firmly anchored political solidarity among the
constituent units, the separation of economic and political institutions
may not be necessary; but in Africa the advocates of continental or
subcontinental political union are likely to achieve more success via
economic than political integration. On the other hand, the establishment of integrated unions implies considerable limitations on national
political freedom of action.

THE CONDITIONS FOR SUCCESSFUL REGIONAL
ECONOMIC INTEGRATION

The mere desire for economic integration and the establishment
of regional or subregional units themselves cannot guarantee the
success of African unions. Unless the countries composing a union
permit the free movement of goods and services and labor and capital,
the integrated economy cannot last. Economic activities within the
region or subregion must be harmonized with respect to such matters
as tariff and trade policy, monetary, fiscal, and investment policies,
and transport and communications networks, which permit goods and
services to be moved quickly within the larger market. Furthermore,
meaningful unions can be established only if they are accompanied
by a policy of social reform and justice, administrative efficiency,
and political stability of the member countries. To the extent that
most of these prerequisites are lacking in many African countries,
the prospects for successful regional or subregional integration are
dim.

It is essential that the benefits of integration be distributed equitably among the component countries, particularly as imbalances in the levels of development exist. Indeed, it is the unequal development among the various parts of the same country that gives rise to tensions, secessions and threats of secessions, and political instability. In the absence of conscious efforts to correct such imbalance, integration may contribute to more pronounced differences among the member countries of the union. Measures that might be taken to minimize the adverse effects of integration in the less-developed members include temporary protection of their imports and exports through the imposition of a differential tariff or the subsidy of exports, preferential access to markets, trade reciprocity and the granting of fiscal incentives and state aids to enterprises wishing to settle in these parts of the union, compensation for revenue losses and fiscal transfers, the improvement of infrastructural services, and a systematic promotional effort designed to stimulate the sectors that can make a dynamic contribution to the rapid economic development of these areas.*

REGIONAL GROUPS IN NON-AFRICAN DEVELOPING COUNTRIES

Latin America

As mentioned earlier, the attempts at integration in the developed countries have encouraged similar attempts in the developing countries. In 1961, under the Charter of the Alliance for Progress, the Latin American countries, together with the United States, committed themselves to the economic integration of the region. Arising from the efforts of the Alliance and those of the U.N. Economic Commission for Latin America (ECLA), all the Latin American countries belong either to LAFTA or to the CACM. **

---

*In the East African Economic Community, the advantageous differential rate of growth of Kenya via-à-vis the rest is causing a gradual lessening of the spirit of cooperation among the members of the community, each of which is trying to pursue its own national economic program.

**Most Latin American commentators on the alliance have noted its slow rate of progress as compared with that being made by Cuba, one of the few Latin American countries outside the alliance and outside LAFTA and CACM.

In the Caribbean, a free trade area exists between Guiana, Barbados, and Antigua (population, 0.6 million). The CACM, established in 1952, consists of Costa Rica, El Salvador, Honduras, and Nicaragua (population, 12 million). Trade barriers on almost all items were abolished in mid-1967. They maintain a uniform tariff toward nonmember countries on about 98 percent of the tariff items, employ a means of allocating industries and rationalizing industrial location, harmonize fiscal policy, and establish common institutions, such as the Central American Integration Bank, a bank clearing house, and an industrial research institute. The intra-CACM trade increased from about £3 million in 1950 to about £60 million in 1968. About 70 percent of the intra-CACM trade now consists of industrial products. [12]

LAFTA is composed of eleven countries—Argentina, Bolivia, Brazil, Chile, Colombia, Ecuador, Mexico, Paraguay, Peru, Uruguay, and Venezuela (population, 180 million). They have granted a large number of tariff concessions to one another, and intensive studies have been conducted on the means of harmonizing tariff and trade policies toward nonmember countries and of reducing further the remaining trade barriers. The central banks of the member countries established a reciprocal credits and a clearing system in 1965. Intra-regional exports and imports have considerably increased. Because of the endemic political instability in Latin America, however, these measures have not given rise to any noticeable rapid economic growth.

The Middle East

Even though the Arab countries in the Middle East have the same religion and civilization, economic cooperation among them has been negligible. In 1953, most of the countries signed a convention that provided for a 25 to 50 percent tariff reduction on certain manufactured goods. In 1964, they agreed to establish an Arab Common Market ACM, which is to be fully consummated on January 1, 1974.* The agreement provides for a 20-percent tariff reduction on almost all manufactured goods and a 40-percent reduction on agricultural products on intra-ACM traded goods. Quantitative restrictions have been abolished on all the industrial and agricultural products on which tariff reduction operates. Studies are being conducted on the establishment of a common external tariff and the harmonization of development plans. [13]

---

*Jordan, Lebanon, Saudi Arabia, Syria, and Kuwait (population, 16.5 million).

South and East Asia

The trade among the South and East Asian countries is about 30 percent of their total trade—that is, larger than in Latin America, the Middle East, or Africa. But progress in regional cooperation has been slower and more limited than in the other three regions. Apart from the preferential arrangements that exist among the British Commonwealth member countries of the area, there are two existing subregional economic groups. One, the Association of South-East Asia, created in 1961, consists of the Philippines, Thailand, and Malaya (population, 70 million), and aims at cooperation in economic, educational, and scientific fields, including joint industrial projects and a free-trade area in selected products. The other, the Regional Cooperation for Development agreement (RCD), set up in 1964, consists of Iran, Pakistan, and Turkey (population, 160 million). The countries have established institutions for the improvement of the infrastructure of member countries, joint shipping services, the study of the distribution of key industries, and the removal of intra-RCD tariff barriers. But intra-RCD trade, mostly in petroleum, is less than 2 percent of the total value of the region's trade. The Economic Commission for Asia and the Far East (ECAFE) is encouraging regional cooperation mainly through the establishment of the Asian Development Bank.

AFRICAN REGIONAL GROUPS

East African Economic Community

Of the existing unions in Africa, the most important is the East African Economic Community (EAEC). The genesis of the community dates back to the colonial period. In 1917, a customs union was established between Kenya and Uganda, and in 1920 Tanganyika became a member. A common external customs tariff was introduced in 1922, customs tariffs were eliminated in 1923, and the duty-free transfer of imported goods between the countries was established in 1927. [14] The joint customs administration set up between Kenya and Uganda in 1917 was not extended to Tanganyika until 1949. Common income tax rates, structures, and administration have been maintained since 1939, after which joint agricultural, industrial, and medical research organizations were established, in addition to common operations in civil aviation, meteorological services, railways, harbors, airways, ports and telecommunications, and a university for East Africa. The East African Currency Board was established in 1919, and up to 1966, when central banks were established for each of the countries, the union maintained a common currency; a high degree of monetary integration still exists among the three countries.

During the period of monetary union (1919-66), there was free mobility of currency and capital. No restrictions existed on the mobility of labor and employment before 1966, when Kenya introduced legislation requiring work permits from noncitizens, including those from the union. A common Central Legislative Assembly (CLA) was established in Nairobi, Kenya, in 1948 when the East African High Commission, composed of the governors of the three countries, was introduced. The members of the CLA were appointed partly by the governors, partly by the unofficial members of the legislatures of each country; its jurisdiction extended over the common services.

Until 1961, the High Commission lacked independent sources of revenue and had to be financed by contributions from the unit territories, while most of the common services were self-financing. But, in 1961, the recommendations of the Raisman Fiscal Commission led to the establishment of a Distributable Pool Account, designed to provide an independent revenue for the union.* When Tanganyika became independent in 1961, the High Commission was transformed into the East African Common Services Organization (EACSO), with an executive authority consisting of the premiers of the three countries. The authority operated through committees composed of ministers from each country. The decisions of the committees could be implemented only if there was unanimity. The common market itself was not established until 1967, when the heads of state of the three countries signed the treaty that provided for the EAEC.

The administration of customs and excise of the community is handled by the East African Customs Department, which is part of the EACSO. Although the structure of the tariff is determined by the CLA, the rates are enacted separately by each of the national legislatures. There are at present only minor exceptions to complete uniformity in customs duties. Until 1964, there was also total uniformity in excise duties. In that year, Tanzania imposed a consumption tax on beer, and in 1966 Uganda imposed first the same tax and later extended it to a wide range of goods produced outside Uganda, while also adjusting upward tariff rates to protect locally produced goods. Today, differential consumption taxes exist among the three

---

*The Raisman Distributable Pool Formula originated in the defunct Central African Federation of Rhodesia and Nyasaland in the late 1950s. It was introduced into the Nigerian Federation by Sir Jeremy Raisman in 1958.

countries with respect to hotel taxes, airport charges, and motor vehicles. [15]

Income taxes are similarly administered by the East African Income Tax Department, which is also a part of EACSO. The tax structure is determined by the CLA, but the rates and allowances are enacted separately by each government. Uniformity has virtually been achieved with respect to personal income taxes and corporation taxes, but not with respect to export taxes. [16] Since 1965, however, Tanzania and Uganda have introduced supplemental development levies over and above the uniform tax base.

The revenue collected from customs duties accrue to the country of final destination and, from excise, to the country of origin of the commodities. The revenue collected from personal income taxes is allocated to the country of residence of the payee, and from companies that operate in more than one country on the basis of derivation—that is, the country where the revenue is earned. In order to redistribute tax revenues so as to offset the inequalities arising from the principle of derivation, a Distributable Pool Account was established in 1961-62. Under the account, 94 percent of revenue collected from customs and excise and 60 percent of corporation taxes are allocated on the basis of derivation, described above. After deducting the cost of collection of the revenue, 50 percent of the account is used to finance the common services and 50 percent is allocated equally among the member countries. [17]

Intracommunity trade in 1962 amounted to about 42 percent of total trade, mainly in manufactures. Three quarters of total trade originated from Kenya, as industry within the community has tended to concentrate there. On attaining independence, the other two countries tried to rectify the imbalance by allocating certain industries on the basis of need and by introducing temporary quotas on imports from surplus countries to enable deficit countries within the community to increase their productive capacity. Because of the disputes that arose as a result of the imbalance, the common currency arrangements were terminated in 1966, and the continuation of the community has been threatened since 1967. [18] In that year, however, a new treaty establishing the EAEC was signed. The treaty provides for the widening of the community and includes Zambia, Malawi, Ethiopia, Burundi, and the islands of Mauritius and Madagascar in the union.

The existence of the community almost led to the federation of the three original members in 1963, but the intention fell through, mainly because of fear of the domination of Kenya and the ebullience of socialist Tanzania. Even though integration has not gone as far as was intended and hoped, however, the community has enabled East

Africa to become a unified market, increased the tempo of industrialization in the territories, brought about an enhanced rate of economic
growth comparable with that attained by many of the advanced countries
(though the rate of growth has not been uniform, being higher in Kenya
than in the other two), led to increased specialization and production
efficiency in the community, enlarged the market available to each of
the member countries, increased the pool of skilled labor in the area,
and increased the flow of domestic and foreign capital and skill to
East Africa.

The major problem of the community has been the uneven distribution of the gains of integration. The Kampala Agreement of 1964,
directed in part at eliminating economic imbalances among the members, provided for the following:

1. That certain industries operating in more than one country
increase their activities in Tanzania or establish new ones there

2. That quotas be introduced on exports from the surplus countries to facilitate the building up of productive capacity in the deficit
ones

3. That the surplus countries should increase their purchases
from the deficit partners

4. That a committee of industrial experts be appointed to survey
long-range problems of allocating industries among the three countries
and the provision of a system of differential incentives to attract
manufactures into the less-developed parts of the community.

Equatorial and North Africa

The next in order of importance and effectiveness to the EAEC
is the Equatorial Customs Union (UDE),* which consists of the Congo
(Brazzaville), Gabon, the Central African Republic, Chad, and the
Federal Republic of the Cameroons. In 1910, the Federation of French
Equatorial Africa was established among the first four countries, with
a governor-general and a high commission in Brazzaville. It provided
common services such as defense, transport, posts and telegraphs,
collection and disbursement of customs duties, and the guiding and
management of the economies of the four territories. During the
colonial period, the union was administered as a highly centralized

_____

*Union Douanière Equatoriale.

federation under a federal grand council, but as the individual countries approached independence, the federation was loosened. In 1957, most of its functions were transferred to the individual territorial governments. By 1958, they became autonomous republics within the French community, and by 1960 they became fully independent but associated members of the union. [19]

In 1959, the four members signed a convention providing for the preservation of the customs union and the operation of agreed common services—rail and river transport, posts and telegraphs, customs administration, coordination of internal taxes, and common currency and monetary policy. It also provided for the replacement of the high commission by central agencies. The Republic of the Cameroons joined in 1961. In 1966, the union was strengthened by a new treaty that established the Customs and Economic Union of Central Africa.*

The decision-making body of the union consists of the Conference of the Heads of States, which acts on unanimity and approves decisions and programs to be legally enforced in each of the states. There is a common external tariff for all items, a common investment code, and a common central bank. A part of the customs duties collected is paid into a solidarity fund, which is redistributed to compensate the inland countries for the customs duties they lost as a result of their geographical position and, as members of the union, of their sacrifice of the power of imposing customs duties. The members consult closely on the establishment of industries, and the excise duties collected are allocated according to the share of products consumed by each country.** The levels of import duties and indirect taxes are decided by a joint committee, which also harmonizes the various taxes within the domestic jurisdiction of the member states.

The union has enjoyed a common monetary system since 1940. With the establishment of the Central Bank in 1960, it has been able to centralize its external reserves, to guarantee freedom of movement of currency and monetary transfers within the union, to adopt common rules for foreign-exchange transactions, bills of exchange, checks, and the control of credit, and to operate a common currency.

In the field of industrial harmonization, Chad and Cameroon agreed in 1963 on the establishment of a cement factory in North

---

*Union Douanière et Economique de l'Afrique Centrale.

**Twenty percent of the import duties and taxes are paid into the solidarity fund and the balance allocated among the units.

Cameroon to supply the needs of the two countries. A similar cement factory was established in Libreville, Gabon, a spinning and weaving factory in Chad, a bleaching and printing works in Cameroon, a sugar factory between Brazzaville and Pointe Noire in the Congo, and a common oil refinery in Port Gentil, Gabon. The customs union provides for the free movement of persons, goods, services, and capital among union members as a means of harmonizing development plans. Export industries and industries serving the market of only one member country could be set up in any of the member countries without reference to the union, while all other industrial projects must be scrutinized and their location approved by the Central Committee of the union.

The Entente* was established in 1959 and has succeeded only in setting up a mutual aid and guarantee fund for external loans. It is primarily a political grouping, but it also provides for the harmonization of development plans. The common fund benefits the less-developed members of the union more than the rest. Ivory Coast, the richest member, contributes the lion's share and draws little or nothing from the fund. As an economic unit, the Entente has not been a significant success.

The Maghreb Union has set up a Permanent Consultative Committee to coordinate development plans and to study systematically the basis of common policies and practices with respect to trade, industry, transport, communications, tourism, statistics, and budgeting. A center for industrial research has been established in Tunisia. A common export policy is being formulated and a joint petroleum policy is under study. There is a plan to reduce internal trade barriers, but, at present, primary goods move freely within large areas of Morocco, Algeria, Tunisia, and Libya, although intra-Maghreb trade amounts to only 5 percent of the total value of the trade of the member countries.

The South African Customs Union

The South African customs union is one of very unequal partners. It is both a common market and a customs union, between the Republic of South Africa and Lesotho, Botswana, and Swaziland. It is a currency union with closely linked banking and financial institutions. A substantial part of the labor force of the three smaller and poorer countries is employed in the mines of the Republic of South Africa. There are also close links in transport and services.

The union came into existence in 1889, when the Cape Colony and the Orange Free State established with the other British colonies

---

*Conseil de l'Entente.

in South Africa a customs union and a free-trade area and accepted the policy of distributing the customs duties collected in the area equitably among the four British colonies of the Orange Free State, Cape Colony, the Transvaal, and Natal. When, in 1910, a political union of the four provinces of South Africa came into being, the terms of the union were abrogated and a new one between the new Union of South Africa and Basutoland (Lesotho), Bechuanaland (Botswana), and Swaziland was signed in June, 1910. The agreement provides for the maintenance of the customs union until it is changed by the Republic or any of the union members; the free interchange of South African products and manufactures between the Republic and the territories; the payment by South Africa to the territories of a fair share of the customs duties collected on locally produced goods passing through the ports of member countries; and conformity by the territories to the tariff laws of South Africa.[20] Since the agreement, a high proportion of the trade of the three territories passes through South African ports, and South African products dominate the internal markets of the union.

Communications and services are integrated, and road, rail, telephone, telegraph, and international air services operate through South Africa. Because of the dominance of South Africa, no appreciable industrial development has taken place in the other three member countries, as industrialists find the market within South Africa less risky. The only few major industries outside the Republic have been established in Swaziland. The major agricultural export goods are marketed through South African marketing boards. It is obvious that the terms of association between South Africa and the three territories are greatly determined by political factors, and the other black African countries view closer ties of those territories with apartheid South Africa with disfavor.

West Africa

The history of West Africa is the history of various attempts at integration. It started by conquests and statecraft and by the spread of ideas from one region to the other. The empires of the Sudan, Ghana, Mali, Soughay, and the Jihads merged large areas of independent kingdoms into one. In 1920, the West African National Congress, which met at Accra, with delegates from all British West Africa, advocated a union of West African countries. It has been shown above how the French colonial authorities assisted in integrating their eight colonies in West Africa into a customs union. Britain, through the establishment of a common currency, research institutes, and common transport and communications agencies, tried to assist in the integration of its West African colonies. Although the British colonies are interspersed with non-British ones, yet colonial link sustained the common services until each of the countries became independent. It was Ghana that first broke away from the common services, and each unit has followed suit. It can readily be said that economic integration is least developed and least seriously advocated among the former British colonies of West Africa.

In 1966 and 1967, however, the articles of association for a West African Economic Community, to embrace both former British and French West African countries and Liberia, were considered in Niamey and Accra, respectively. The treaty, which emphasizes more political than economic links, even if ratified, will be less effective than any of the unions already described. In fact, the recent economic measures in Ghana and, to a lesser extent, in Sierra Leone, whereby West Africans were compelled to withdraw from specific trades and leave the countries, for whatever cause, are antiintegration measures.

The French West African Customs Union was established in 1959. No duties are collected on trade among the member countries, and the revenues from import duties on goods purchased from outside the union are redistributed equitably among the countries. But customs barriers still exist among most of the countries, although a few of them have harmonized their trade relations. Products originating in the countries and goods manufactured internally continue to move freely, although independent actions on taxation and economic policies have reduced the effectiveness of the union. There have been attempts since 1967 to establish a common external tariff and to distribute the revenue on an agreed basis.

The only other recognizable attempt at integration in West Africa is that between Gambia and Senegal, which in April, 1967, signed a formal treaty of association. The aim is to promote and expand cooperation and coordination of economic activities in all fields; but, while Senegal favors political as well as economic integration, Gambia prefers to retain its autonomy. As a result, only a defense agreement has been ratified.

The African Development Bank

A common aspect of most of the integration measures in Africa is that most of the unions are only at the stages of discussion, study, and interstate negotiations. There is general desire, however, particularly outside the British West African countries, for monetary and fiscal integration to be achieved through an African clearing and payments union, the formation of an African monetary council, and an African monetary center of studies and cooperation. Although no significant measures have been taken to promote such cooperation on a continental scale, the African Development Bank was established in 1964. The All-African People's Conference in Tunis in 1960 had passed a resolution calling for an investment bank to promote development projects. In 1962, the ECA undertook to plan the establishment of the bank, and by 1963 twenty African governments had ratified the plan. To date, almost all independent African countries are member participants of the bank.

THE PROBLEM OF THE SIZE OF
REGIONAL GROUPINGS

The wider the area and the market, the greater are the benefits of economies of scale, specialization, and bargaining power. It is mainly because of these that larger unions have been advocated around the world. It is also true that the more countries involved in forming a union, the more difficult it becomes to reach agreement on unified action and eliminate internal trade barriers and external trade differences, as the case of Africa illustrates. The geographically smaller groups, like the original three-member East African Economic Community and the Equatorial Customs Union, originally more successful than the others, became less so with the addition of new members to the union. Also, the smaller the countries, either as individual members or as a composite unit, the more urgently the necessity for union is appreciated.

On the other hand, too many separate groups within the same region or subregion tends to split the area into unnecessarily competitive and exclusive economic groups. Conflicts arise owing to mutual discrimination between the groups and between neighboring countries that belong to different groupings; the tariff barriers of each group might prevent mutual trade advantages. In order to prevent these disadvantages, it might be desirable that the subregional groupings have superimposed on them a general regional or continental framework, providing for a preference and a reasonable level of reciprocity among the groups. Alternatively, all the countries in the continent might agree to designate specific industries and joint economic activities that will operate regionally or continentally for optimum efficiency, while still keeping the various groups for the purposes of less continent-wide economic projects. One of the problems of large economic units is efficient management. Particularly in Africa, where commercial, industrial, and administrative management is not as efficient as it should be even with respect to the handling of local and national economic enterprises, a continent-wide union might be nothing but a window-dressing and an invitation to greater economic inefficiency. The examples of the publicly owned statutory corporations in Africa have not given encouragement to even the greatest advocates of Pan-African economic measures.

Since the unions are governmentally determined and operated, a translation of the local inefficiency, corruption, and mismanagement into wider economic unions might slow down the rate of economic growth. As even some of the smaller unions already described, like the Equatorial Customs Union, extend over 12 million square miles—the equivalent of the area of Western Europe—the problems of effective and rapid contact among the component units must be fully appreciated if the union is to be efficiently administered in the absence of ideal transportation and communication links.

CONCLUSIONS

Although the gains of the various attempts at integration in Africa have been small, they represent the eagerness with which it is becoming increasingly realized that a wider political and economic integration is desirable. Economic integration cannot, however, succeed to any major extent unless there is also a strong degree of political unity, which implies the surrendering of national sovereignties by many of the independent African countries. It appears that few African countries are willing to surrender their political autonomy and independence to a larger union. This general attitude has turned even the OAU into a debating forum for the independent African countries. Clearly, individual economic and political nationalism is on the ascendancy, growing out of the long struggle of the nations to consumate their newly won political freedom. Integration would appear to be more effective if emphasis were placed along the lines suggested by the Economic and Social Commission of the OAU, which apparently have been taken lightly, if at all.

The experiences of the EAEC are worth emulating in other regions of Africa, but it must also be remembered that the political and economic nationalism of the individual countries in East Africa is becoming a danger to the continuance and effectiveness of the EAEC. As each of the three territories began to plan its economy separately and to solicit external aid independently, interstate rivalries grew in the industrial sphere. It must be stressed, however, that much of the existing integration was forged by the colonial powers during their control in Africa, and their influence is still behind most of the existing integration proposals.

There are external and internal dangers to effective regional integrations in Africa. The developed countries that had colonies in Africa and that still divide the now-independent countries into spheres of influence and markets attract many of the latter into the former metropolitan economic relationships. Thus, the French African countries look more toward France for meaningful economic collaboration than toward Africa. The former British colonies behave similarly. The North and Northeast African countries behave more Arabic than African, while some countries in Central and Southwest Africa are gradually being drawn into the vortex of the South African economy. The whole idea of associating African countries with the EEC demonstrates the strength of the pull of the colonial legacy. Since in many African countries the main policy advisers are expatriates from the excolonial countries or their associates, the pressure toward integrating with Europe rather than with neighboring African countries is even increasing. The various incentives being given by individual African countries to attract European and American investors and the stronger emphasis on foreign aid, even with encouragement by the U.N., constitute a threat to regional integration in Africa.

Internally, the various different language groups into which Africa has been divided tend to impede integration, particularly when these language groups are not geographically contiguous enough to form viable and homogeneous economic unions. The different monetary systems, the similarity of the various African economies, all of which are essentially agricultural and not trade-creating, the different levels of development, and the fact that many of the individual countries themselves are not internally integrated but are plagued with rival ethnic and subethnic difficulties make regional integration difficult to attain.

Also, it is doubtful if there are enough mature and dedicated African political leaders who can administer wider political and economic areas than they are at present managing. Africa is a continent wherein the educated and technically competent citizens become civil servants, teachers, and employees of foreign-owned enterprises, while the oftentimes less competent and less Pan-Africanist colleagues run the governments, decide policies, and ultimately mismanage the economy, the country, and the continent. A survey of the indigenous Africans who are full-time agricultural, industrial, and commercial entrepreneurs will show clearly that they are not the educated and technically competent, but the illiterates and drop-outs—without whom, nevertheless, the economic development in Africa today would not have been achieved.

There is the added problem of the dominance of foreign enterprises in the African economies, particularly in the industrial field. Many of the economic advantages of integration benefit foreign rather than African industrialists. About 80 percent of the large-scale industries in Africa are owned by foreign concerns, which are the first to receive loans from the commercial and development banks that are being set up.* Also, it is predominantly the same foreign-owned enterprises that benefit from the investment incentives that almost all African countries are being urged to provide to attract foreign capital and develop increased domestic participation. 21

It is therefore important that one of the objectives of increased economic integration in Africa be an increased domestication, nationalization, and Africanization of the economy, particularly with reference to mining, oil exploration, iron and steel, and other key industries. This implies that more and more Africans with the techno-logical, managerial, and orientational skills should participate more and more in the actual production, distribution, and exchange of goods and services in Africa.

---

*For instance, in Nigeria, about 90 percent of the loans granted by the Nigerian Industrial Development Bank (NIDB) since its estab-lishment in 1964 have gone to foreign-owned industries. Early in July, 1970, the federal government issued a directive that 80 percent of such loans should henceforth be granted to Nigerian-owned industries. The Industrial Research Unit of the Department of Economics, University of Ife, has discovered that out of about 6,000 Nigerian-owned industries of all sizes, fewer than 20 have got any bank loans. Not one has got a loan from the NIDB.

NOTES

1.   United Nations, Economic Commission for Africa, African Economic Indicators (Addis Ababa, 1968), Table VI. The population of the African continent was thus estimated at about 226 million in July, 1967.

2.   It was estimated that in 1000 the GDP of Brazil alone was equal to 50 percent of the GDP of all the African countries. The GDP of the U.K. alone was 2.5 times greater; of the U.S.S.R., 6 times; of the United States, 19 times. (African Economic Indicators, p. 15.) In Africa, only 9 countries have a population exceeding 10 million each; 29 have less than 5 million each, 13 of which have less than 2 million each.

3.   See Tibor Scitovsky, Economic Theory and Western European Integration (London: Allen and Unwin, 1962), pp. 15-16.

4. See United Nations, Trade Expansion and Economic Integration Among Developing Countries, Report by the Secretariat of UNCTAD (New York: United Nations Conference on Trade and Development, 1967), pp. 6-10, also, P. N. C. Okigbo, Africa and the Common Market (London: Longmans, 1967), Ch. 7, pp. 137-57.

5. United Nations, A Contribution to Economic Integration Policy in Latin America, E/CN 12/278, 1966, pp. 99-116.

6. See Hollis B. Chenery, "Patterns of Industrial Growth," American Economic Review, June, 1960, p. 264; and Peter Robson, Economic Integration in Africa (London: Allen and Unwin), Ch. 7.

7. C. A. Cooper and B. F. Massell, Towards a General Theory of Customs Unions for Developing Countries (Santa Monica, Calif.: Rand Corporation, May, 1965), Ch. 1.

8. United Nations, Direction of International Trade (New York, 1968).

9. The Republic of South Africa constitutes the largest single market in Africa. In 1966, South Africa accounted for about 8.6 percent of the population and 24 percent of the GDP of Africa as a whole. (African Economic Indicators, p. 16.)

10. See "Bank of Sierra-Leone: Economic Trends," (Freetown: September-October, 1969), pp. 1-3.

11. Scitovsky, Western European Integration, pp. 44-46.

12. See United Nations, The Latin American Common Market and Economic Bulletin for Latin America, 1965, pp. 127-62. See also Carlos Manuel Castillo, Growth and Integration in Central America (Madison: University of Wisconsin Press, 1965).

13. See Trade Expansion and Economic Integration Among Developing Countries, p. 18.

14. Peter Robson, Economic Integration, Ch. 4, pp. 97-165.

15. Ibid., p. 107.

16. Ibid, p. 108.

17. Ibid, pp. 113-14.

18. B. F. Massell, Economic Union in East Africa: An Evaluation of the Gains (Santa Monica, Calif: Rand Corporation, September,

1964); Arthur Hazlewood, "The East African Common Market," Bulletin of the Oxford Institute of Economics and Statistics, 1966.

19. V. Thompson and R. Adloff, The Emerging States of French Equatorial Africa (London: Oxford University Press, 1960), Ch. 1-3.

20. Robson, Economic Integration, pp. 254-55.

, 21. Of the 148 industries that enjoyed investment incentives in Nigeria between 1958 and 1969, only the smallest two were Nigerian-owned. See S. A. Aluko, "Fiscal Incentives for Industrial Development in Nigeria," U.N. Study (Vienna: UNIDO, 1968); and "Incentives for Industrial Development in Nigeria" (Vienna: UNIDO, 1969).

First Participant: The idea of regional economic groupings was now universally accepted, and one hoped that such groupings would one day exist throughout the world. In Africa, the debate was whether these groupings should be confined to political and linguistic areas, or whether they should transcend these barriers and embrace ecological and geographical zones. Decentralization of the processes of the same industry among several countries of a regional grouping would entail many difficult problems, particularly with regard to the procedures for allocating certain processes to individual countries, the sharing of profits, and the movement of labor within the decentralized industry. The key to economic integration was the coordinated planning of packages of complementary industries that could be allocated among the members of the grouping. For this to be achieved, dissemination of industry and economic development within the union would have to be such as to prevent any one country or political group from dominating the union.

Second Participant: One of the obvious advantages of regional economic groupings was the greater possibility of facilitating cooperation in joint research projects embracing various ecological zones. Economic integration would also demand an examination of the disparate educational systems of the various linguistic zones of Africa, with a view to achieving some uniformity and, particularly, adapting education to actual needs.

Third Participant: While the advantages of regional cooperation were self-evident, one did not bring about economic integration by merely drawing lines across the map of Africa to establish regions of cooperation. A lot more would be required in terms of the perception and willingness of leaders to forego the short-term advantages of autarchic planning for the long-term benefits of African economic development. The main problem was to communicate these judgments to the decision-makers in government.

Fourth Participant: Scientists and scholars could take the lead in the movement for regional cooperation by initiating regional research projects without waiting for government initiatives. In this connection, it would be desirable to consider those areas of cooperation that would lead to the quickest results.

Fifth Participant: Only Africans themselves must determine

the form of their own institutions as a necessary condition of achieving their national and regional objectives. As a practical demonstration of the desire for cooperation, there might first be the abolition of visas among African countries by a meeting of the heads of state of the OAU.

Sixth Participant: With regard to the flow of interunion services, there could be difficulties arising from national aspirations that demanded the provision of a service without reference to contiguous countries. The speaker pointed out that as a result of the unilateral declaration of independence by the minority white regime in Rhodesia, resulting in the interdiction of petroleum products to Zambia, it was decided on short notice to construct a pipeline and railway between Lusaka and Dar-es-Salaam, on the Indian Ocean, as a cooperative enterprise between Tanzania and Zambia, a decision that should prove beneficial to both countries.

Seventh Participant: The success of regional integration would depend on the availability of capital to initiate multinational projects, and, while the African Development Bank was designed primarily to encourage such projects, unfortunately it had been handicapped by lack of technically competent personnel to evaluate projects, make financial studies, or explore new projects. In effect, the Bank had been more of a savings bank than a development bank.

First Participant: It was the dependence on foreign capital (of the 11.5 million pounds the Bank had for lending, 9.5 million came from the World Bank) that was hindering African development. The main effort would have to be made by Africans in Africa for Africa, as reliance on external assistance for success was unrealistic and illusory.

Eight Participant: A method of mobilizing domestic capital which had been tried successfully in the U.A.R. involved the issue of ten-year development certificates bearing interest at 5 percent. In two years, these certificates had all been bought up and the government had raised 1 billion pounds from domestic sources for national development. This was the kind of experiment that might be tried by the African countries.

First Participant: The problem of manpower in economic development was one of upgrading productivity, of making African labor more efficient. There was need for specialized training, in addition to formal education, geared to the needs of the country's development priorities. Tied to the problem of productivity was the question of adequate rewards for labor; governments should be prepared to offer appropriate rewards to attract the needed skills within the economy.

Ninth Participant: A project in the Congo aimed at providing training for various categories of employees had one serious drawback: after training, the employees naturally expected promotion or increased remuneration, and when this was not forthcoming, they left the industry, to be replaced by untrained and less-efficient labor. Wages, therefore, constituted an important factor in the upgrading of productivity.

Third Participant: The problem of the misapplication of trained manpower, particularly in the public service, could be the result of the suspicion with which politicians viewed civil servants. Perhaps this suspicion could be overcome if civil servants belonged to the ruling political party. On the other hand, this might detract from the essential role of the civil service as the evaluator and implementator of government policy. Clearly, the role of the civil service in new nations demanded careful examination.

Tenth Participant: In most discussions on African economic development, no attempt had been made to establish a rationale for development, and until there was such a rationale, consistent with the African's own needs and aspirations, African countries would continue to pursue economic policies inherited from the former colonial regimes—policies designed to enhance the exploitation of colonial resources for the colonizing power. A sound, realistic economic policy was indispensable to the formulation of the kind of development program that had the chance of raising the quality of life for the masses. Here, the question of incentives was crucial. Frequently, it had been assumed that the low productivity of the rural masses was necessarily owing to the lack of skills or to the unawareness of new techniques of production. It appeared more likely that the problem was one of a lack of incentives. After all, the Ghana cocoa industry had rested on the productivity of the individual peasant producer— some 900, 000 of them—who, without any dramatic technological advances in production methods, had made Ghana the dominant producer of cocoa in the world in just seventy years. The problem of incentives was, of course, not confined to the price the farmer received for his output; it related to the whole condition of rural life and what the masses could expect from increased effort. With regard to the problem of rural out-migration, there was a quaint notion that the solution was to introduce agricultural subjects into the curricula of the rural school and thus keep the drop-outs "on the farm. " The reason for the exodus from the countryside had very little to do with curricula; it had much to do with the unutterable dullness of the rural existence. Thus, the changes required to keep them "on the farm" must be related to improvement in the quality of rural life.

Ninth Participant: Development was for the human being, and must begin and end with him. Indeed, realization of the human

potential in society was of the highest importance and should be re-
warded with the greatest amount of welfare accruing from the development process. Thus, if today Africans walked on foot, it was
hoped that tomorrow they could ride.

The conclusion of the symposium was devoted to an overview of the discussions and the distillation of the consensus achieved on the issues that formed the major preoccupation of the participants.

DISARMAMENT

1. The main reasons for African arms expenditures were seen to be concern for internal stability, the incidence of border problems, and anxieties generated by the problem of South Africa in particular and southern Africa in general. It was considered that arms build-up in Africa would be reduced if greater attention were paid to the resolution of political problems through negotiation.

2. It was illusory for African countries to expect that disarmament by the great powers would release resources for international development. African countries should realize that they would have more resources for development if they made reductions in their own arms budgets.

3. The developed countries should be called upon to desist from encouraging African countries to arm by offering military assistance through sales or grants. The role of the armaments industry in promoting the build-up of arms and in discouraging disarmament in all countries was strongly deprecated.

4. A military confrontation with South Africa could not as yet be contemplated as a means of settling the problem of apartheid. For the present, measures likely to have some effect included the support of freedom fighters and pressure of various kinds on the friends of South Africa to induce them to use their influence, economic and otherwise, to persuade South Africa to reverse its policies.

5. The symposium rejected the arguments advanced by the
United Kingdom to support its decision to resume the sale of arms to
South Africa.

6. African countries should not regard large military establishments as a means of establishing international status and prestige,
but should be aware of the danger of the military gaining a dominant
position in nonmilitary spheres of national activity.

7. While it was appreciated that conditions in certain countries
had necessitated the intervention of the military in political affairs,
in general it was considered undesirable that the military become the
guardians of political institutions and agents for the guarantee of good
government.

SCIENCE, TECHNOLOGY, AND DEVELOPMENT

1. There should be a central scientific council responsible for
determining national science priorities and for allocating resources
to these priorities. The council should be independent of any particular
government department or ministry, but should have close links with
the government agency responsible for the planning of economic and
social development.

2. Membership of the council should be broadly based and
interdisciplinary, including representatives of relevant government
departments and ministries, industry, commerce, universities, and
research organizations. There should also be representatives of the
main branches of scientific and technological activity, including the
social sciences. In appropriate cases, nomination of members to
represent scientific disciplines should be entrusted to learned societies
and professional associations.

3. The council should have adequate funds at its disposal, and
under its control, for the support of research and development in
institutes, universities, and other organizations and for other relevant
activities.

4. The council should enjoy a reasonable degree of stability
and freedom from political interference to ensure continuity in the
pursuit of its programs.

5. At this stage in the development of African countries,
research, whether fundamental or applied, should preferably be
oriented toward the solution of local problems. Attention should be
given to adaptive research as a means of utilizing the existing reserves
of knowledge in the developed, as well as in the African, countries.

6. The problem of manpower for science and technology had to be tackled right from the lowest levels of the educational system. Scientific ideas must be introduced in primary school in order to counter, among other things, the prevalence of traditional attitudes and beliefs and in order to make the pupils receptive during their later years to further scientific education and training. There should be adequate emphasis, at this and at the secondary-school levels, on the use of modern methods of science teaching and on practical work.

7. At the higher levels, provision should be made for training not only scientists and technologists, but also technicians. Technological education at all levels must be modern and up to date.

8. Postgraduate training must be oriented to produce personnel capable of tackling local problems.

9. In order to attract persons of sufficient caliber, the scientific and technological professions should enjoy status and have career structures and expectations equal to those in other types of employment.

10. Adequate funds and manpower were needed for the task of translating research results into economically beneficial projects. The modernization of agriculture through the adoption of scientific methods deserved special attention.

11. One of the most important areas of the application of science and technology, for the advancement of African countries, was the utilization of natural resources, based on thorough surveys and careful planning.

12. Industrialization should take into account the special economic and sociological circumstances of each country. Special emphasis deserved to be given to industries utilizing local raw materials or satisfying local needs, including the needs of agricultural modernization and of other essential industries.

13. Other areas deserving attention were improvement in health, including the eradication of communicable diseases, the elimination of malnutrition, and the provision of better environmental sanitation and of social services; and improvements in transport and communications.

14. There was a need for regional specialized centers of research to tackle the common problems of countries in the same region. Such centers need not be restricted to countries with common political orientation or belonging to groups linked by a common language.

15. Other useful forms of regional cooperation would involve the exchange of personnel between research centers in different African countries, the exchange of information, and the training of personnel, required by one country, in another African country or in regional centers.

16. There should be a place for the training of specialists under the auspices of international organizations.

17. Scientists had an obligation to educate the authorities in their countries to have confidence in their qualified nationals and not to trust only the advice of outsiders.

18. There was a need for integration in the efforts of physical, biological, technological, and social scientists at seeking solutions to national problems.

ECONOMIC DEVELOPMENT

1. The aim of development must be to improve the quality of life of the ordinary man.

2. An important determining factor in the development of any African country was the quality of its human resources. In this regard, it was essential to reorganize the entire educational system to reflect more closely the needs of the African countries. In this, the systems in neighboring countries, fashioned after the French or British educational models, should be examined together, in an effort to produce systems suited to the common needs of the countries.

3. There should be more effective planning in the utilization of trained manpower to promote development.

4. Effective development required that economic activities be undertaken and controlled by Africans. There was a need, in this connection, for African countries to develop self-reliance.

5. In order to ensure that development had its origins in local effort, more attention should be given to methods of raising capital in the African countries themselves. There should be the cultivation of self-discipline and the avoidance of extravagance on the part of both governments and individuals.

6. Regional economic groupings were desirable as a first step to wider groupings embracing the whole continent. Regional groupings could be approached from cooperation at such levels as the improvement

of communications and transportation within the region and integration arrangements in the fields of trade and tariffs, money and banking, and social legislation. Other measures were the rationalization and integration of industrial activity within and between countries and the promotion of free movement of persons across frontiers through the abolition of visas and other restrictions.

7. It was essential to increase the flow of services—transportation, communications, and so on—between regional groups or between different parts of the continent, the provision of the facilities being a factor that would generate an increase in the demand for such services.

FORMATION OF AN AFRICAN REGIONAL PUGWASH MOVEMENT

It was considered that the coming together of independent scientists and scholars from various African countries to discuss the problems of the entire continent had been useful and that steps should be taken to promote the convening of similar symposia with wider representation from countries in the different linguistic zones. A proposal was adopted to seek the authority of the Continuing Committee of the Pugwash Conferences on Science and World Affairs to establish an African Regional Pugwash Group, with the participants of this symposium as a nucleus. Professors O. Bassir and F. G. Torto were nominated to act as joint convenors and to endeavor to gain the support of suitable persons throughout the continent. They were also to act as coordinators of any future proposals for the holding of symposia, pending the formation of the full group and the election of officers. It was decided that the conclusions of the symposium should be distributed to the following: African universities; association of African universities; academies of sciences; selected scientists; heads of governments; research organizations; planning commissions or ministries of planning; ministries of foreign affairs; science policy councils; ECA, UNESCO, OAU, and ECOSOC (U.N. Economic and Social Council); and other appropriate individuals and organizations.

ALUKO, Samuel A.

Professor of Economics
University of Ife
Ife, Nigeria

ARKHURST, Frederick S.

Director of African Programs
Phelps Stokes Fund
New York, N. Y.

BASSIR, O.

Professor of Biochemistry
University of Ibadan
Ibadan, Nigeria

CARNEY, David

Director
United Nations Institute of
    Economic Development and
    Planning
Dakar, Senegal

DE GRAFT JOHNSON, J. C.

Professor of Economics
University of Ghana
Legon, Accra, Ghana

EL-BEDEWI, Fathi

Professor of Physics
Ein Shams University
Cairo, U. A. R.

GINGYERA-PINCYWA, A. G. G.

Lecturer in Political Science
Makerere University
Kampala, Uganda

GOMA, L. K. H.

Professor of Zoology
University of Zambia
Lusaka, Zambia

ISHAG, H.

Professor of Chemistry
University of Sudan
Khartoum, Sudan

MAZUMDAR, H. K.

UNESCO Visiting Professor of
    Economics
University of Ife
Ife, Nigeria

NGOIE, J.	Lecturer in Economics
	Institute of Economic and
	    Social Research
	University of Louvanium
	Kinshasa, Democratic Republic
	    of Congo

POLK, William R.	President Adlai Stevenson Institute of International Affairs Chicago, Illinois
OLADAPO, I. O.	Professor of Engineering University of Lagos Lagos, Nigeria
READ, James M.	Charles F. Kettering Foundation Dayton, Ohio
TEKLE, Asefa	Director Imperial Central Laboratory Institute Addis Ababa, Ethiopia
TORTO, Frank G.	Professor of Chemistry University of Ghana Legon, Accra, Ghana
WASAWO, D. P. S.	Professor of Zoology University of Nairobi Nairobi, Kenya
YANNEY-EWUSIE, J.	Professor of Botany University College Cape Coast, Ghana

FREDERICK S. ARKHURST is Director of African Programs at the Phelps-Stokes Fund, New York. He was formerly Director of African Programs at the Adlai Stevenson Institute of International Affairs in Chicago. He also served as principal secretary of the Ghana Ministry of Foreign Affairs and as head of the Ghana Foreign Service, and was Ambassador-Permanent Representative of Ghana to the United Nations. Mr. Arkhurst has lectured and written on African politics, economic development, and international relations, and has directed courses in diplomacy on behalf of the United Nations Institute for Training and Research. He is a consultant and Senior Advisor to the Secretary-General of the United Nations Conference on Human Environment. Mr. Arkhurst is editor of Africa in the Seventies and Eighties: Issues in Development (Praeger, 1970).

SAMUEL A. ALUKO is Professor of Economics and Head of the Department of Economics at the University of Ife, Nigeria. Dr. Aluko is a member of the Nigerian Economic Society, the International Association of Public Finance. He is Chairman of the Mid-West State Tax Board of Nigeria, and is also a member of several public source bodies in Nigeria, including the National Advisory Committee on Statistics and the National Council on Industrial Research. Professor Aluko has written extensively on Economic Development and Public Finance.

DAVID CARNEY is a consultant from the United Nations Economic Commission for Africa to the East African Community and was formerly the Director of the United Nations Institute for Economic Development and Planning, Dakar, Senegal. Dr. Carney has held teaching posts at Lincoln and Fairleigh Dickinson universities, the University of Ibadan, the University of Ghana, and Antioch College. His publications include Government and Economy in British West Africa (1961), Patterns and Mechanics of Economic Growth (1967).

A. G. G. GINGYERA-PINCYWA is a lecturer in Political Science at Makerere University, Kampala, Uganda, and has published a number of articles on African politics.

L. K. H. GOMA is Vice-Chancellor of the University of Zambia, Lusaka. Dr. Goma is a distinguished entomologist, with considerable teaching and research experience in government, at the universities of Ghana, Makerere (in Uganda), Zambia, the Ross Institute of Tropical Hygiene, the London School of Hygiene and Tropical Medicine, and the East African Virus Research Institute. Dr. Goma is Chairman of the National Food and Nutrition Commission, Zambia, and Chairman of the Scientific Council of Africa, Organization of African Unity, and has a long association with the Pugwash Movement on Science and World Affairs. He has published several papers and communications in scientific journals and two books, The Mosquito (1966) and Ngoza na Kaswa (1962).

ALI A. MAZRUI is Professor of Political Science, Makerere University, Kampala, Uganda. Dr. Mazrui has held teaching appointments at the universities of Oxford, Chicago, and California. He has lectured and written extensively on African politics and his publications include Towards a Pax Africana (1967) and Ancient Greece in African Political Thought (1967).

FRANK G. TORTO is Professor of Chemistry and Dean of the Faculty of Sciences, University of Ghana, Legon, Accra, Ghana. Dr. Torto has a long association with the Pugwash Conference on Science and World Affairs and is a leading advocate for the establishment of an African Regional Pugwash Committee. He has lectured extensively on science and development.